First Hand

- making the Foundation Curriculum work

First published in Great Britain in 1998
as 'First Hand – a quality curriculum for the under fives'
by The Featherstone Education Partnership.
Reprinted 1999

This edition, fully revised, published
by Featherstone Education Ltd, 2001
Reprinted May 2002

Text by Sally Featherstone with additional material by Alison McInnes
Photographs by Gary Clarke and Alison McInnes
Illustrations by children from Wyvern Primary School, Leicester
Edited and designed by Phill Featherstone

ISBN 1-902233-54-9

Featherstone Education Ltd
44-46 High Street
Husbands Bosworth
Lutterworth
Leicestershire LE17 6LP
United Kingdom
(++44) (0)185 888 1212
www.Featherstone.uk.com

Contents

This book is intended to help all those who work with children in the Foundation Stage, in planning, managing, assessing and evaluating a curriculum based on first hand experiences and play. It aims to support them in guiding and organising children's learning to meet the national expectations described in the *Guidance for the Foundation Stage* published by QCAin 2000.

Where we refer to **teachers** we include all qualified practitioners in the establishment. We also use the words **school, nursery, setting and establishment** to cover the wide range of provision for children under six in maintained and independent sectors.

The advice given is based on extensive consultation with people who work with young children. While we consider it represents the best of current practice it will, of course, be subject to local requirements and the needs of individual establishments.

Introduction
Why we need to identify the early years curriculum

The characteristics and needs of three, four and five year olds are unique. They reflect a wide ranging stage of development, part of a continuous period of rapid growth and change which does not begin to slow down until after the age of six. Interest in the early years curriculum has increased as the National Curriculum has developed, as the Foundation Stage has been identified, and as varying provision has evolved for children who have not reached Year 1.

An appropriate curriculum for children of this age provides experiences which acknowledge age, maturity and different capabilities, while building upon the existing knowledge, skills, understanding and attitudes which children bring to any learning. In order to achieve this a clear definition of the Early Years curriculum, its organisation and management is vital.

In 1985 HMI suggested nine areas of learning and experience which they considered the essential framework of education for all children, including the under fives. These were –

- aesthetic and creative
- human and social
- linguistic and literary
- mathematical
- moral
- physical
- scientific
- spiritual
- technological

(*The curriculum from 5-16*, HMSO 1985)

In 1996 the then Schools Curriculum and Assessment Authority (SCAA) produced a publication called *Desirable Outcomes for Children's Learning*. The *Desirable Outcomes* combined the nine areas of learning to form six areas of experience. This did not involve a reduction in breadth, but brought together related headings:

- personal and social development (previously moral and spiritual)
- language and literacy (previously linguistic and literary)
- mathematics (previously mathematical)
- knowledge and understanding of the world (previously human and social, scientific and technological)
- physical development (previously physical)
- creative development (previously aesthetic and creative)

In 2000, the Qualifications and Curriculum Authority, after extensive consultation with practitioners and early childhood experts, published guidance which clarified the curriculum to be offered to all children who have not yet reached the end of Reception year.

　　　　First Hand – making the Foundation Curriculum work

The publication *(Curriculum Guidance for the Foundation Stage),* not only identifies learning goals for the end of the Foundation stage, but gives clear guidance on the stages of development towards those goals and the ways in which practitioners should support development and influence the quality of children's learning. It also states that 'the word curriculum is used to describe everything children do, see, hear or feel in their setting, both planned and unplanned'. The national guidance uses the six areas of learning as a framework for planning and assessing the curriculum for children in the Foundation Stage (from 3 to the end of Reception).

In this book we demonstrate that a broad, balanced curriculum and a clear set of learning goals are not incompatible with a curriculum based on play and first hand experiences. We offer practical advice on the construction, management and monitoring this curriculum which not only acknowledges the needs of very young learners, but also enables children to make progress towards achieving the *Early Learning Goals,* preparing them appropriately for statutory education in Key Stage 1.

We begin by looking at the principles of early years education and the needs of very young children. It is necessary to identify the curriculum for the Early Years so that we can ensure that the principles which have been agreed are translated into practice, meeting the needs of children at a crucial stage in their development.

In Chapter 2 we explore the process of defining the curriculum, and include a curriculum map based on the work of a group of Early Years practitioners. This map could form a part of the policy for any establishment catering for children under and around the age of five, and Chapter 3 contains a framework for constructing such a document.

Chapter 4 covers starting points and baselines, and the use of information gathered to construct teaching and learning plans for individuals and groups. We have included current examples from schools to illustrate these processes, and link these to the guidance from QCA.

Chapter 5 investigates the role of adults in the setting. The practitioner who works woth the children, and the other adults who support her.

Chapter 6 addresses the complicated task of managing the Early Years curriculum within the context of the whole school; the challenges which face governors, headteachers and senior managers, teachers and their assistants.

Chapter 7 deals with the wealth of advice, information and help available from parents, the local community and specialist services.

Finally, in Chapter 8 we confront the continuing need for monitoring, evaluation and review. We offer practical advice on conducting internal self review, and on preparing for and managing inspections.

The areas can be combined in a variety of ways, but the result should be a curriculum which:
- *is broad, balanced, differentiated and relevant*
- *takes account of the assessment of children's progress*
- *promotes equal opportunities*
- *responds effectively to special needs*
- *promotes the spiritual, moral, cultural, mental and physical development of the children*
- *prepares pupils for the opportunities, responsibilities and experiences of adult life*

Education of Children under Five, HMSO 1989

Managing the intentional curriculum

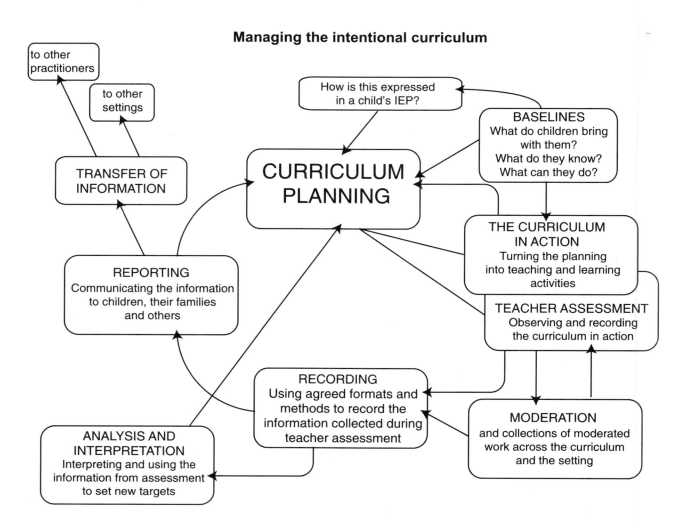

This diagram charts the relationship between the various processes of providing an intentional curriculum, each of which is discussed in later chapters.

First Hand – Making the Foundation Curriculum Work is a new version of the book first written in 1998. Like the previous version, it is written for professionals working in a demanding field. Time is precious and the questions we raise do not have simple or quick answers. Each chapter is intended to stand alone as a focus for discussion, and many groups will continue to explore the contents over a period of time. To help you, we have prepared two additional elements in the *First Hand* programme, companions to this book.

First Hand – auditing the curriculum for the Foundation Stage is an interactive guide in two parts. The first part, based on Chapter 3 of this book, leads you through the stages needed to construct a policy for the Early Years, helping you to turn the *First Hand* principles into practice as well as to meet your legal obligations. The second part provides a template for self evaluation which establishments can use to check the quality of their provision, perhaps in preparation for inspection. It is available in book form, or as a computer disc for you to customise and print in your own versions.

Delivering quality provision at any stage of education is a difficult and complex task. This is nowhere more true than in catering for three to five year olds. Your response, as individuals and as teams, must reflect your appraisal of your own situation and your stage of development as an organisation. You must choose how you approach this book and its associated materials, and the route you will take through them.

Managing the pace of change is critical to the success of your ongoing development as a school, nursery, pre-school or group; you know where to start and how fast to go! Remember that your situation is unique; its uniqueness reflects the needs of all the individuals involved, first and foremost those of the children in your care.

> 'We now have the scientific evidence, from brain studies and child development work, to know that three to six year olds learn by doing.'
>
> Wendy Scott, Chairwoman of The British Association for Early Childhood Education (BAECE), quoted in The Times Educational Supplement, March 1998.

LUKE

Chapter 1
Principles
and
needs

In 1989 the then Secretary of State for Education set up a Committee of Inquiry under the chairmanship of Angela Rumbold to look into the quality of the educational experience offered to three and four year olds. A year later the Committee produced its report, which it called, appropriately enough, *Starting with Quality.*

The report was significant in a number of ways, particularly in its analysis of issues relating to Early Years practice and in its recommendations for achieving high quality provision for all under fives. It had considerable influence on establishing the notion of a national entitlement curriculum in the Early Years, which evolved alongside the development by OFSTED of the processes of inspection, and the introduction of the nursery voucher scheme.

Some five years after the publication of *Starting with Quality* the Schools Curriculum and Assessment Authority (SCAA), since absorbed into the QCA, produced some equally important guidance. The SCAA recommendations built upon the major features of the Rumbold report with an important addition. It defined what it called 'desirable outcomes' which stated, very succinctly, what children should be expected to know, understand and do in order to embark upon the first stage of the National Curriculum. The desirable outcomes were mapped against the six areas of experience, and the advice was that 'the (Early Years) programme must ensure progress towards the desirable outcomes in each area of achievement.' (*Nursery Education Scheme - The Next Steps*, SCAA 1996). The nursery voucher scheme, which the *Desirable Outcomes* were intended to underpin, has gone, but the outcomes themselves remained in place until 2000 as a useful national framework for planning the curriculum for the under fives.

In 2000, following extensive consultation, the QCA and the, as it then was, DfEE produced further guidance on the pre-statutory curriculum. The guidance document introduced a new key stage (the Foundation Stage) which would come before Key Stage 1. This stage was to apply in all settings receiving Government funding, and would extend to the end of the reception year. The need to ensure continuity between the Early Years curriculum and the first stages of compulsory education had been an ongoing concern for those who worked with younger children, and there is now general agreement that an appropriate curriculum for the Early Years should have clear and well articulated links with the National Curriculum. Also there is a recognition that there will be some overlap with Key Stage 1 programmes of study, since some children will already have competencies within the Key Stage 1 range. The Foundation Guidance addresses all these issues. Key Stage 1 now starts at the beginning of Year 1, and the confusion surrounding the reception year has finally been resolved.

Principles

The model of the curriculum described in this book is based upon eleven guiding principles, which we believe should underpin all curriculum planning for under fives. They are –

1. **The child is at the centre of decisions about the curriculum.**

The Early Years curriculum is as strongly affected by legislation and national initiatives as the other stages of education. However, it is worth emphasising at the outset that decisions made by Foundation Stage providers should be based upon the needs and best interests of the children who attend.

2. **The curriculum should reflect the way young children learn, preserving the place of play, talk and first hand experiences.**

Children learn by doing: by exploring, playing, negotiating, watching, copying and demonstrating. They make sense of their learning by talking about what they are doing, and they internalise it by reviewing, through language and other forms of expression, what they have done. We must meet these needs by making sure that the curriculum gives children a wide range of opportunities for play, talk and exploration with many different materials in a variety of groupings and situations.

3. **It is important to take account of the child's previous learning and the next steps in achieving his or her potential.**

In order to turn the curriculum into effective practice, it is necessary for the adult to make informed judgements about the existing knowledge, skills and understanding which the child brings to the pre-school environment. This should inform decisions about what the starting point should be for cohorts, groups and individuals, and will enable the setting of targets for future learning.

4. **The curriculum for the Early Years is an intentional curriculum which can and should be defined.**

The Early Years curriculum cannot be left to chance. Adults working with young children need to be clear about what they are providing, why and how, and to have clear intentions about the outcomes for the children. They should identify what needs to take place within the six areas of experience in order to build on what children have done and learned, and to prepare them for the future. Within this framework the adult can use professional expertise to fine tune activities to meet the needs of each individual child.

5. **The curriculum must be planned to ensure coverage, continuity and progression.**

Effective planning should ensure that each curriculum area is sufficiently covered and prevent inadvertent omissions. Plans should ensure that the starting point for children is identified through baseline assessment. Continuity and progression within the curriculum should be addressed through planning and links with other educational settings, to ensure that practitioners are familiar with the expectations and experiences of age groups other than those which they currently teach.

'Play is indeed the child's work.'

The Nursery Years,
Susan Isaacs,
Dent 1929

'Children are entitled to learn through their senses and physical activity, through active involvement in first hand experiences and play ...

...and to be supported in their learning by practitioners who plan and organise an environment, indoors and outdoors, for active learning, physical movement, first hand experiences, creativity and play.'

Quality in Diversity in Early Learning,
Early Childhood Education Forum 1998

6. The child has right of access to a planned curriculum which reflects and meets all needs.

Having defined and planned the curriculum, care must be taken to see that it is available to everyone. It must be expanded, adapted and modified to ensure that all children have access to the activities offered. In addition, there is a need to monitor, and to intervene where necessary to ensure that, over time, planned intentions and outcomes are met.

7. The curriculum for under fives demands trained, experienced, knowledgeable staff.

Adults who work with young children should have training which is relevant to the age group. This may be from a period of initial training but could also be through a structured process of in-service professional development. The most effective practitioners will want to ensure that they stay up-to-date through regular exposure to experiences outside their normal work which will broaden their knowledge and understanding of children and how they learn. The role of an Early Years practitioner is highly skilled and complex. It requires a knowledge of child development and the curriculum, together with the ability to organise and support learning. It is also physically and mentally demanding. Practitioners need to be able to review and reflect on their practice and to refresh their thinking and approach.

8. There is a need for the informed selection and use of appropriate materials and equipment.

Materials and equipment play an important part in the presentation of the curriculum to the under fives, and therefore in the learning which develops from the activities provided. Resources do not have to be elaborate or expensive; in fact it is often better if they are not, because simple things frequently work best. However, careful thought and planning are needed to ensure that resources available support the achievement of the learning intentions, and that they are easily accessible to adults and children.

9. The presentation of the curriculum should enable children to learn how to learn.

Care should be taken to see that children understand tasks, know what is expected, why, and how this helps their learning. The way in which the curriculum is presented to young children determines the degree of independent thinking which can take place, and therefore the extent to which the activities offered will stimulate the development of confident and successful learners. Learning about learning helps children to make sense of the curriculum.

10. Learning happens in a variety of settings, groupings and situations

There is no single or foolproof recipe for success. Children learn in a variety of ways and different individuals flourish in different contexts.

First Hand – making the Foundation Curriculum work

Some will shine in group work, others may prefer to work alone. And the same child may respond to the same learning situation differently on different days! This makes the planning of learning opportunities and outcomes very difficult. The task of the adult is to be sensitive to the needs and preferences of the child while creating a balanced range of opportunities for learning. In choosing which objectives are to be the focus of the learning, the adult must decide how best to organise the activity for each of the individuals involved in order to achieve their intentions for learning, while at the same time remaining flexible, and responsive to children's emerging needs and interests.

11. Learning is subject to many influences, some of which are beyond our control.

Time, adult support, home circumstances, society and the media, health, the influences of other adults and children are all factors which are usually beyond the teacher's control. We need to be clear about the ways in which we can bring about children's learning so that we are not distracted by things we can do little or nothing about. Of course, we should be aware of and sensitive to the possible effects of these influences, but it is important that we concentrate our energies on the elements which we *can* affect, and for which we are trained.

To sum up, an effective curriculum for the Early Years should be based on an identification of the needs of young children in order to ensure accessibility to appropriate, first hand learning experiences, moving on from the home environment and providing continuity with later statutory provision.

What are these needs?

The developmental needs of young children are many. They are also varied and complex, but they may be broken down into four main areas which have a bearing on the early years curriculum. These are cognitive development, physical development, social development and emotional development.

For cognitive development children need –
- a range of first hand, practical experiences providing opportunities to explore and investigate
- to re-visit, to practise and consolidate
- a range of methods of presentation and materials
- time to pursue and extend spontaneous ideas which develop from natural curiosity
- activities and equipment appropriate to their stage of learning and development
- to work in different ways at their own pace
- to learn from mistakes and take risks
- realistic challenges
- feedback about their learning

Six areas of the curriculum, four areas of need

cognitive development

physical development

For physical development children need –

- access to safe indoor and outdoor environments, with space to move freely and expend energy
- to practise and develop coordination of gross and fine motor skills
- time and space to be noisy or quiet, to concentrate and to listen

social development

For social development children need –

- to interact in a variety of different situations with adults and children - one to one, in pairs, in small and in larger groups
- opportunities to develop and maintain relationships with others
- to be recognised and valued as an individual
- to have support for growing competence, enabling them to recognise and respect their own needs and the needs of others
- a range of opportunities for purposeful talk and listening

emotional development

For emotional development children need –

- an emotionally safe environment where they can develop understanding of routines and boundaries
- praise, encouragement and positive reinforcement
- opportunities to develop independence
- the security of approval and acceptance, and to be valued as an individual
- to make choices and decisions and to take responsibility

The object of a planned and intentional curriculum for the under fives is to present a range of learning experiences which will meet these needs. How such a curriculum can be provided, organised, resourced and managed is the subject of the chapters which follow.

Summary

- The curriculum for the Early Years is unique. It therefore can and should be defined.
- Any curriculum for the Early Years must take into account the wide range of abilities, experiences and aptitudes of children of this age.
- The curriculum must be firmly based on agreed principles.
- The curriculum must acknowledge the specific needs of young children for cognitive, physical, emotional and social development.

Chapter 2

Defining the Early Years curriculum

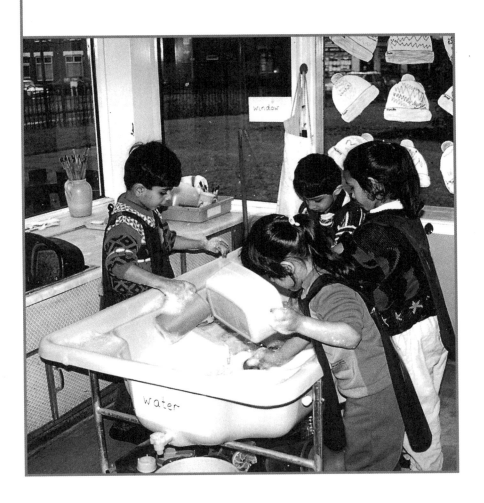

What is a curriculum?

A school curriculum is a map of experiences and opportunities. It identifies *what* should be taught – the entitlement experiences for all children – and gives reason and form to the teaching and learning offered. It covers the principles and areas of learning, includes the content or programme of study, detailing which experiences should be offered, when and how, with suggested methodology, organisation, resources and activities. It takes the aims of the establishment and begins to translate these into practice, providing the long term objectives for planning and teaching. It also states the intended outcomes for children at different stages of their experience.

So what then, is a curriculum for the Early Years? - bearing in mind that children in the Early Years may be in a school, but may also be in a wide range of other settings. The curriculum for the Early Years forms the first stage of the formal learning programme. It covers any period before Year 1, and includes the whole reception year. It should, therefore, encompass children in pre-schools, nurseries (in both the maintained and independent sectors), reception classes, as well as reception age children in mixed age classes. In this chapter we explore the definition of a curriculum for the Early Years which sets out the entitlement for each child, what it should contain and where it should lead.

Barbara Tizard (*Early Childhood Education*) talks of a curriculum which is 'intentional'; that is, a curriculum which is planned, has clear objectives and is supported by thoughtful methodology. An intentional curriculum is based on care and first hand experiences, and is closely linked to the home. These are, of course, vital elements of the Foundation curriculum. However, we must recognise that we also have a responsibility for the intellectual development of children, and for preparing them for the next stage of education, at the beginning of Year 1.

The six areas of experience, the Stepping Stones and the *Early Learning Goals* (see the Introduction and Appendix 1) offer a common platform for individual schools and other pre-five settings for planning, teaching and assessing the Early Years curriculum. They also provide an essential link between the pre-statutory curriculum and the programmes of study for Key Stage 1.

Any curriculum must be firmly rooted in the setting's aims and should follow the principles established by the practitioners. It should take account of local and national advice and requirements, providing a framework for teaching and learning and the recognition of success. The policy document and the accompanying curriculum map are public statements of the setting's intentions. Their purpose is to ensure that curriculum entitlement is clear to everyone. They need the support of all who have a stake in the school, and so should result from discussion and common agreement between staff, governors, parents and advisers.

For ease of use, the curriculum in a school is usually divided into *stages* and *subjects* or *areas*. For instance, most primary curriculum documents

---

'The curriculum of the nursery school can hardly be distinguished from that of the home... both parents and teachers provide the same kind of learning experiences for a child but the teacher formulates her objectives and has theories about her methods.'

Early Childhood Education, Barbara Tizard, NFER 1974

'The teachers of under-fives need to know the curriculum attainment targets and programmes of study for the first Key Stage, 5-7, so that the experiences they provide for children take them towards, and in some cases cover, the early parts of the work. Equally infant teachers need to know what children have learned in the nursery and plan the work to take account of the stage the children have reached.'

The Curriculum from 5-16, DES 1994

are now broken down into key stages or double year groups, and into the subjects of the National Curriculum. The Foundation Stage Guidance now clearly indicates that all settings (including schools) should adopt the areas of learning as a description of the elements of the curriculum for the Foundation Stage.

Early in this book we introduced the curriculum structure promoted by the QCA since 2000, based on six areas of learning and experience. These areas are now used nationally for planning, organising, assessing and inspecting the Foundation Stage. We take these areas as the foundation and starting point for the curriculum map on the following pages.

- **Personal, Social and Emotional development**
  Learning how to work and play, co-operate and function in a group, develop personal and moral values, understand self and others.
- **Communication, Language, and Literacy**
  Talking, listening and encouraging children to become readers and writers.
- **Mathematical development**
  Mathematical understanding and the foundations of numeracy, with a focus on practical mathematics.
- **Knowledge and understanding of the world**
  Finding out about the world around, other people and features of the natural and man made world. These become a foundation for history, geography, technology and science.
- **Physical development**
  Physical control, mobility, awareness of space and manipulative skills in indoor and outdoor environments. Establishing positive attitudes towards a healthy and active way of life.
- **Creative development**
  The growth of imagination, and the ability to communicate and to express ideas and feelings in creative ways.

The QCA *Early Learning Goals* provide a range of outcome indicators for the curriculum. They are signposts pointing out the direction for the journey and identifying the point which children should reach by the end of Reception. They are not a curriculum in themselves.

The *First Hand curriculum map*, which follows, has been developed from work done by a group of Early Years teachers and nursery nurses during a series of workshops in Leicestershire. It builds on the six areas of learning, and by incorporating practitioners' own knowledge and experience develops them into comprehensive guidance, combining national expectations and the needs of the children in a manageable and child-friendly structure.

'The curriculum offered by a setting comprises the full range of experiences, opportunities and activities which are planned to promote children's learning.'

Looking at Children's Learning
SCAA 1997

The *First Hand curriculum map* is organised like this –

Learning Outcomes

A range of **outcomes** for each area, including and extending from the Early Learning Goals. These are the expectations for children at the point when they are ready to embark on the National Curriculum programmes of study for Key Stage 1. This point of readiness may occur at any time during the Foundation Stage.

↓

Key experiences

The **key experiences** which form an entitlement curriculum, and lead to the goals – a core of essential experiences, which may be extended by the setting or individual practitioners.

↓

Suggested activities

A wide range of **suggested activities**, situations and opportunities which deliver the key experiences. This is not an exhaustive list and practitioners will certainly wish to add to it.

↓

Resources

A survey of some of the essential **resources** needed to provide and support the curriculum described.

Please note that the *First Hand curriculum map* covers **content and activities**, not **methods or organisation**. There are many ways to organise and provide this curriculum. Some of these are explored in Chapters 5, 6 and 7.

Summary

- The curriculum for the Early Years reflects the aims of the school. It forms the first stage in the whole school curriculum plan.
- The curriculum for the Early Years should be intentional – with clear objectives across all areas of learning and experience.
- The curriculum document states long term objectives and entitlement (what should be offered and experienced).
- The curriculum for the Early Years should include intellectual, social, personal, physical and creative development.
- The *Early Learning Goals* and the *First Hand curriculum map* offer a structure for providing and managing quality experiences for children.

Please note

The *First Hand curriculum map* consists of six sections, one for each of the areas of experience. It is arranged on double pages for ease of reference.

1. Linguistic & literary development

Outcomes at age 5 in knowledge, skills, understanding and attitudes

Early learning Goals

* enjoy listening to and using spoken and written language, and readily turn to it in their play and learning
* explore and experiment with sounds, words and texts
* listen with enjoyment and respond to stories, songs, and other music, rhymes and poems and make up their own stories, rhymes and poems
* use language to imagine and recreate roles and experiences
* use talk to organise, sequence and clarify thinking, ideas, feelings and events;
* sustain attentive listening, responding to what they have heard by relevant comments, questions or actions;
* interact with others, negotiating plans and activities and taking turns in conversations;
* extend their vocabulary, exploring the meanings and sounds of new words;
* retell narratives in the correct sequence drawing on the language patterns of stories;
* speak clearly and audibly with confidence and control and show awareness of the listener, for example by their use of conventions such as 'please' and 'thank you';
* hear and say initial and final sounds in words, short vowel sounds within words;
* link letters and sounds, naming and sounding all letters of the alphabet;
* read a range of familiar and common words and simple sentences independently;
* know that print carries meaning, and in English, is read from left to right and top to bottom
* show an understanding of elements of stories, such as main character, sequence of events, openings, and how information can be found in non fiction texts, to answer questions about where, who, why.
* attempt writing for various purposes, using features of different forms such as lists, stories, instructions
* write their own names and labels and form sentences, sometimes using punctuation
* use their phonic knowledge to write simple regular words and make phonetically plausible attempts at more complex words;
* use a pencil effectively and hold it effectively to form recognisable letters, most of which are correctly formed;

Additional outcomes

* knows about different kinds of print in the environment
* uses a growing vocabulary with increasing fluency
* uses marks, letters, symbols & familiar words to communicate meaning
* can write independently (emergent writing) e.g. in role play
* knows that language must be appropriate to the situation
* can speak clearly, audibly & with appropriate range of volume
* is confident to speak & eager to contribute
* is aware of & respects other languages
* knows that in English, print goes from left to right & top to bottom
* understands that books are for everybody
* can share books & look at a book alone

Key experiences to build the above

Children should have opportunities to experience –

* a literature & print rich environment
* purposeful talk & reasons for writing
* role models of adults as readers & writers, speakers & listeners
* a wide variety of literature, rhymes & songs in different forms from different cultures, settings & times (including fiction, non fiction, pictures, tapes, video, etc.) & in different groups
* letter writing
* live performance
* other forms of text – tapes, posters, labels, magazines, comics, lists & recipes
* interaction with others, adults & children
* quiet areas for reading & writing
* a wide range of songs, rhymes & stories
* a variety of forms of text
* a wide range of materials, equipment & surfaces for mark making & writing
* a variety of purposes & contexts for writing & reading
* handling books
* using puppets

& opportunities to –

* speaking, listening & stories in groups ranging from 1:1 to whole class
* communication with other children & adults in English, mother tongues & other languages
* activities which develop pride in own & others' work
* activities which develop manipulative skills with a variety of tools & techniques
* share books with peers & adults
* make a range of responses to texts - drama, drawing, collage, etc.
* develop listening skills - being an audience as well as having an audience
* retell stories, real & imagined & to use their mother tongue with support where possible
* practise the skills of handwriting & letter formation
* engage in role play, drama & dramatic/imaginative play, including visiting theatre companies & theatre visits
* be heard and responded to
* see their own names & other familiar words in print, on labels, notices, etc.
* see people writing & write their own stories, poems, letters, lists, etc.

Activities

- small group discussion – stimulus pictures, etc. sharing books & taking them home
- story time, stories from pictures, "show & tell", shared reading
- listening to stories, big books, songs & rhymes, including those with repetitions & choruses, or multiple copies of stories
- making their own books, class stories & poems, assemblies
- teacher or older child scribing for their stories
- matching, sorting & other pre reading games
- paired reading, big books, retelling stories
- newspapers, scrapbooks & magazines – picture & word collections
- small sand trays & boards for writing
- visits from authors, book week, visits to book shops & libraries
- book & toy libraries with tapes, puppets, pictures & word games, some in community languages.
- listening to tapes made by children, teachers & other adults (in English & other languages)
- listening walks
- recording own stories & children's voices
- drawing, tracing, writing,
- developmental writing area with equipment for making own labels & notices for models, pictures
- post box, post office
- looking at, discussing & appreciating others work
- teacher as writer & reader (& listener)
- listening to & questioning visitors
- talking about displays; interactive displays

- games, jigsaws, picture & sound lotto, I-Spy, dominoes, play people, road mats, dolls house, feely box or bag
- chalk boards (with chalk & water), white boards, flip charts
- magic stone or shell to pass around group for turn taking
- colouring & other activities to develop fine motor control e.g. dough, Plasticene, threading, peg boards, sand & paint, writing in sand, cornflour, writing patterns, letter shapes (including those in felt & sandpaper), pattern work
- words in displays, around school, on walks
- making books, notices, cards, recipes, lists, labels, notices, posters, invitations, menus, badges, lists – shopping, Christmas, trips, & reminders
- guessing games (e.g. I-Spy); Kim's game & other memory games
- appropriate TV, radio & computer programmes
- displays & sound tables, writing in the school & local environment
- phone pads, appointment books, forms to fill, registers, etc.
- small world play (e.g. Play People, Lego, puppets)
- newspapers, magazines, comics, talk about favourite books
- dramatic play in Post Office, stationers, library, book shop, etc.
- imaginative play in a variety of contexts, acting out stories, familiar events, with materials and stimuli for literacy (e.g. a notebook, appointment book, directory, prescription form)
- looking at & describing objects & artefacts; diaries, weather charts, birthdays

Resources & equipment

- imaginative play areas with relevant resources to introduce change and development
- wide range of books (fiction, non fiction, poetry, etc.)
- stimulus pictures & photos with cultural relevance & gender balance
- tape recorder, tapes & headphones, taped books, telephones, calculators
- visitors & parents to talk to
- comfortable child sized furniture, floor cushions
- registers, diaries, appointment books, forms (for dramatic play – better if unused)
- handwriting patterns, marble rollers, tracing
- dolls house, Lego, small world people
- posters, comics, forms, catalogues
- puppet theatre & puppets, play television
- flat, smooth table big enough for at least two
- display space, open shelves or racks for storage

- writing area with wide range of pencils, felt pens, pencils, charcoal, pastels
- different types of paper in different sizes and shapes, envelopes, tracing paper, home made books, materials for book making
- school made information books and blank ready made books (2 or 3 pages)
- printed or written materials (e.g. calendar, class list, flannel graph)
- notice board, hole punch, paper clips, scissors, rubbers, rulers, staplers, punches, photocopies of names, print from magazines and catalogues etc.

2. Mathematical development

Outcomes at age 5 in knowledge, skills, understanding and attitudes

- can count from 1 to10; do simple practical addition & subtraction in everyday situations
- can copy, complete & make own patterns
- can compare, sort & match according to different criteria
- can use their knowledge to solve simple practical problems
- can work in a pair or group
- can share & co-operate
- can use understanding to solve problems
- can use simple measures
- can select & explore materials such as sand & water
- can use mathematical language in their own play
- can organise equipment, choosing appropriate equipment & using it to solve simple problems
- is co-operative & collaborative
- has experienced larger numbers in real life situations
- shows interest & enjoyment in practical activities
- shows a positive attitude to maths & a willingness to 'have a go'
- is confident with a range of maths activities & concepts & a variety of everyday materials & maths equipment
- asks questions
- respects equipment
- transfers learning to new situations including those out of school

Early Learning Goals
* say and use number names in order in familiar contexts;
* count reliably up to 10 everyday objects;
* recognise numerals 1-9;
* use language such as more, less, greater, smaller, heavier, lighter to compare 2 numbers or quantities
* in practical activities and discussion begin to use the vocabulary involved in addition and subtraction;
* find one more or one less than a number from 1-10;
* begin to relate addition to combining two groups of objects, and subtraction to taking away;
* talk about, recognise and recreate simple patterns;
* use language such as circle, or bigger to describe the shape and size of solids and flat shapes;
* use everyday words to describe position;
* use mathematical ideas and methods to solve practical mathematical problems.

Additional outcomes
- can recognise basic 2D shapes & some 3D shapes & their properties
- is beginning to understand such concepts as size, order, sequence, measure, classify
- knows simple language of position of objects & comparison
- knows a variety of finger rhymes & number games
- knows simple colours & their names
- knows that numbers have names & recognises these as symbols and words
- can sort into sets using simple criteria

Key experiences to build the above

- use the local environment
- create with shapes & numbers
- see numbers & shapes written down
- handle & talk about 2 & 3 D shapes
- develop & talk about spatial awareness
- hear, use & extend mathematical concepts & understanding
- investigate, experience & practise, compare, sort, match, order, sequence
- see & practise number formation in sand, salt, dough etc.
- use everyday objects in such activities as shopping & cooking
- recognise, write & order numbers to 10, & develop awareness of larger numbers
- develop different ways of recording e.g. mappings, sets, pictograms
- talk about maths, ask & answer questions
- enjoy free & structured play & investigations
- work individually & in a group
- hypothesise, predict, estimate & solve problems

Children should have –
- access to a wide variety of practical materials and contexts

and opportunities to –
- explore, develop & use mathematical language in a variety of situations
- experience weighing, measuring, sorting, ordering, comparing, estimating, pattern making, sequencing, problem solving, adding & subtracting, sharing & organising numbers, threading, joining, building (recording their experiences where appropriate)
- record their experiences in a variety of media
- explore & handle real life objects & everyday items (2D +3D)
- observe the use of pattern in everyday life
- use a wide variety of games & maths activities to promote numeracy skills
- experience maths in familiar & relevant contexts
- practise developing skills & concepts
- use maths in different contexts (cooking, shopping, construction, role play etc.)
- use toys & games, board & counting games
- use construction toys & equipment
- develop a sense of pattern
- use information technology, control & data handling
- appreciate numbers in the environment
- use simple operations (+,-) in practical situations
- develop a sense of pattern and rhythm
- talk about position objects & themselves

- hear, join in, act out & learn number songs & rhymes, including those appropriate for outdoors
- number stories (e.g. 3 Bears, Snow White And The Seven Dwarfs, Noah's Ark, The Mouse With Seven Tails)
- maths jigsaws, inset boards, construction toys, puzzles
- ordering activities (e.g. gloves & shoes in pairs, children according to height, families)
- build towers and other constructions with different shaped bricks
- shopping, cooking, setting tables
- a range of number games including those using dice & spinners
- making comparisons through stories (3 Bears, 7 Dwarfs, Titch) & real experiences (e.g. bottles empty & full, heavier & lighter parcels)
- number fishing games, dot to dot, dominoes, bead threading, Unifix patterns
- computer games, calculators, Roamer, Logo
- non standard measures using parts of the body
- turning shapes & tessellation
- sequencing rods & games
- telephones & directories
- cutting & sticking – same/different, smaller/larger than me, small/medium/large
- colour – in role play, home corner
- shape – 2D printing, & 3D blocks
- spatial awareness on outdoor apparatus

- patterns with beads, bricks, children
- sand & water play for capacity, counting, floating and sinking
- 3D shapes, sort for given criteria (e.g. shapes which roll, shapes with curves)
- sequence with beads/Multilink/Unifix/bricks/toys & models/ children/pegboards
- number & shape trails round school
- number writing – in sand, plasticene, dough, paint
- parcels & real objects for balancing; variety of measures for length, volume, time
- register, birthdays, calendar
- matching games & activities – cups & saucers, clothes for dolls, laying the table
- sorting with real life objects, shapes & sorting toys
- role play in shops, cafe, doctor, hospital, hairdresser, etc.
- outside play – chalk games, hopscotch, number ladders, footsteps
- IT programs
- comparisons (to increase vocabulary, e.g. bigger than, longer than, heavier than); estimation of size, weight, etc.
- measuring height of plants, children, growth of pets; simple graphs & charts
- model making with Clixi, Polydron, etc.
- balance on seesaw, scales

- real life objects for weighing, sorting, size, length etc.
- computer, Roamer, etc.
- socks & other clothing for sorting & pairs
- jigsaws & inset boards
- dolls to dress, domestic play equipment (table settings for colour matching, etc.)
- bricks & blocks of different shapes & sizes
- plastic or real money
- sorting toys, logic blocks
- cookery utensils & ingredients
- teachers books from maths schemes
- linking & balancing games - elephants, monkeys, bears
- dominoes, dice, counters, dice games
- matching & sorting games, dominoes
- rulers, tapes, trundle wheels
- laces, beads, buttons
- toy & real clocks

- books and other resources as an ideas bank for the teacher
- books, songs
- calculators
- sand, water with containers, etc.
- scales & balances
- Unifix, Multilink, Dienes, logic blocks, Poleidoblocs
- sorting trays/hoops
- sorting equipment (compare bears, cotton reels, beads, etc.)
- pegs & peg boards
- shop till & equipment
- cooking & craft equipment
- Polydron, Clixi
- solid & 2D shapes

3. Development of knowledge and understanding of the world

Outcomes at age 5 in knowledge, skills, understanding and attitudes

Early Learning Goals

* investigate objects & materials by using all of their senses as appropriate;
* find out about, and identify some features of living things, objects and events they observe;
* look closely at similarities, differences, patterns and change;
* ask questions about why things happen and how things work;
* build and construct with a wide range of objects, selecting appropriate resources, and adapting their work where necessary;
* select tools and techniques they need to shape, assemble and join the materials they are using;
* find out about and identify the uses of technology in their everyday lives and use computers and programmed toys to support their learning;
* find out about past and present events in their own lives and in those of their families and other people they know;
* observe, find out and identify features in the place they live and the natural world;
* begin to know about their own cultures and beliefs & those of other people
* find out about their environment, and talk about those features they like and dislike.

Additional Outcomes

* knows his/her own name, where s/he lives, & the way to school
* knows about different types of weather
* knows that we live in houses, play in the park, buy things in shops
* knows & uses the vocabulary of time – yesterday, today, tomorrow

- can name some body parts, times of day, parts of plants, features of living things
- can select and use equipment and materials for a task
- knows the difference between some natural & man-made articles
- understands that buildings have different uses
- recognises similarities & differences in plants, places & people
- shows interest in surroundings, asks questions 'why?' 'what?' 'how?'
- can talk about & sequence past events in his/her own life
- can talk about observations, explore, predict, question
- can ask questions to gain information
- cares for self, the environment, other people, plants & animals
- is curious/inquisitive & questioning, interested in the environment & living things
- is confident to try out new ideas & activities without fear of failure
- is aware of the world around & how things change over time (e.g. seasons, weather)
- knows where common foods & articles come from
- knows the difference between plants, animals & objects
- investigates pattern & form in nature
- understands the need to care for the environment, e.g. by picking up litter
- understands need for care for living things, e.g. that a plant needs water
- understands that there is a world beyond home and school
- can use scissors and other simple tools to cut, fold, join, build for different purposes
- can explain processes & talk about the things made & done

Key experiences to build the above

Children should have opportunities to –

* explore the classroom & the area in & around the school (the grounds & local community)
* go on visits, walks, explorations
* observe & explore natural & man made objects & note detail & difference
* meet & talk about people, discuss their roles in the environment & community
* observe, sort, describe, reason, make, recognise, conclude
* use all five senses
* use tools & equipment confidently & safely
* appreciate the passing of time & develop a sense of chronology
* experience different cultures, lifestyles, backgrounds, traditions & beliefs
* see, handle & talk about a range of artefacts
* learn in a safe stimulating classroom environment
* appreciate events in the natural world – snow, sun, blossom, rain, leaves, rainbows
* question, plan, prepare & predict, hypothesis, test
* talk about what they have seen, their families & friends, the past, present & future
* respond to stimuli in a variety of ways
* access information from a variety of sources
* use role play equipment

- explore the immediate environment
- use & apply technology & IT
- care for creatures & plants
- choose & use a range of tools & equipment
- make observations & sometimes record them
- cut, stick, join, fold, build, design, plan
- visit places of worship
- develop awareness of the needs of others including animals
- develop understanding of a variety of construction techniques & materials
- design, make & evaluate
- explore, sort, investigate, classify, select materials & their properties
- make constructions
- look after living things
- collect & return materials & equipment to right places
- talk about, describe, touch, taste, smell things
- make simple comparisons
- develop confidence to experiment & hypothesise

- hot & cold cookery to note changes – jelly, meringues, cake, chocolate, recipes from a range of cultures
- forces – outside play, push/pull, up/down
- computer, Roamer
- construction toys & activities
- sewing & collage
- model making with waste materials
- walks & trails round school, grounds, locality (including hall, playground, field)
- cutting out & arranging pictures of furniture in a house
- dolls houses (from different cultures & countries)
- how I have grown, when I was a baby, before I could walk, etc.
- observations of weather
- looking after ourselves – health, hygiene, teeth, food
- exploring our senses – touch, taste, smell, sight – sense tables, feely bags, blindfold games,
- sound tapes, listening walk
- comparisons of then & now
- taking photos of the school & locality
- photos of staff (including premises officer & other support staff), & children – talk about roles & responsibilities
- school plan to find where people work, where things are kept
- investigations (e.g. magnets)

- draw pictures of family & friends
- visits to farms, parks, places of interest
- visitors to school e.g. police, nurse, fireman, grandparents, babies, pets
- baby and other photo displays
- take photos during visits & use later to recall & record experiences
- seasonal experiences – collecting leaves, bark rubbings
- trails & treasure hunts
- construct own street for geography, drama, etc.
- TV & video programmes, CD ROM
- illustrations, plans, maps, labels, notices, instructions
- role play of people's jobs – police, crossing patrol, nurse, doctor
- comparisons – 'when I was a baby', 'when I am grown up'
- plan of classroom, school, neighbourhood
- visits to construction sites, parks during planting, new houses, shops, etc.
- observing & exploring – jelly, cornflour, dough, pasta, chocolate
- forces – through outside play on slides, steps, bikes, etc.
- selected stories using stereotype free images
- growing seeds, incubation, keeping plants & pets
- naming body parts
- cut out collections from magazines, holiday brochures, catalogues

- joining materials - glue. string, tape, elastic bands, stapler
- rigid sheets e.g. card, polystyrene, thin hardboard, plastic trays
- flexible sheets e.g. fabric, paper, cellophane, card
- rods and tubes
- threads and string
- containers
- cleaning materials
- artefacts & objects from home
- construction sets chosen for durability, strength and open endedness in use
- hollow and solid blocks
- accessories e.g. plastic piping, role play props, small scale figures, animals, vehicles
- literacy/maths props e.g. posters, books, maps and atlases, clip board
- large sheets of paper, pencils and felt pens, card, scissors, sellotape, etc.
- clipboards and paper
- shelving for storage
- storage boxes, trolleys, baskets
- a large flat table

- photos, pictures, artefacts
- maps & plans
- anatomy charts & cards
- anatomical dolls
- jigsaws
- tapes recorders & other IT
- photographs, pictures, posters (e.g. from health promoters, school nurse)
- maps & plans
- road layouts, train tracks
- signs and notices
- construction toys & games
- role play materials in theme boxes
- seasonal resources
- mirrors, magnets, measuring tapes, timers, etc.
- construction kits
- maps photo aerial photos, plans
- light sensitive paper
- kites, spinners, windmills, planes
- things that move on wheels, that slide, that float or sink, that magnets will attract
- computer, calculators, tapes & video
- cooking equipment - bowls, spoons, boards, tins, cutters, rolling pins etc
- weather watching - streamers, umbrellas, boots, gloves, magnifying glasses, weather boards etc
- gardening equipment

4. Creative development

Outcomes at age 5 in knowledge, skills, understanding and attitudes

Early Learning Goals

* explore colour, texture, shape, form & space in two and three dimensions
* recognise and explore how sounds can be changed, sing simple songs from memory, recognise repeated sounds and sound patterns and match movements to music
* respond in a variety of ways to what they see, hear, smell, touch and feel;
* use their imagination in art and design, music, dance, imaginative and role play and stories
* express and communicate their ideas, thoughts and feelings by using a widening range of materials, suitable tools, imaginative and role play, movement, designing and making, and a variety of songs and instruments

Additional Outcomes

- knows we have five senses & how we use them
- knows his/her work will be valued
- knows that there are artists, sculptors, musicians, poets & what they do
- knows the difference between pictures, patterns, numbers & letters
- knows that objects, instruments & parts of the body can be used to make sounds & music
- knows that feelings & ideas can be expressed in a variety of ways
- can respond appropriately to stimuli & to his/her own & others work
- can respond to sensory experiences – music, arts, beauty in nature in a range of different forms:
- can use skills in imaginative play

- can participate in a range of role play situations and can take on a character in role play
- can select & use colour, texture, form & shape to express themselves
- can respond to music through dance & to stories through imaginative play
- can use a variety of simple instruments correctly
- can name colours & a range of media; can differentiate between & name sounds, textures and tones
- can hold & control implements & tools, e.g. pencils, paintbrushes, sponges, scissors
- can sing, maintain a simple rhythm, enjoy a range of music
- can organise own workspace, work collaboratively and independently
- can express likes & dislikes & reasons for them
- can move, dance, sing, perform
- can interpret moods in words, sounds, pictures
- is responsive to & able to appreciate beauty, sound, rhymes, music
- is imaginative, enthusiastic, creative, able to experiment
- is aware of safety issues & that some tools are dangerous
- is expressive, confident, spontaneous
- can use knowledge of materials & sounds to create pictures & music

Key experiences to build the above

Children should have experience of –

- a range of groupings for activities from individual to whole class
- a range of mark making tools & surfaces, textures & materials
- a variety of stimuli
- varied opportunities to create pictures, models and constructions
- wide range of types & styles of music, art, dance, stories, pictures, sculptures, etc. from a range of cultures
- a range of different role play situations
- observation, exploration, experiment & discovery through sensory perception using all senses
- frequent access to a wide range of creative materials & resources
- information technology (e.g. drawing & painting programmes)
- activities which develop & support fine motor skills
- wider aspects of aesthetics & creativity in the immediate environment & the world
- working in a pleasing environment
- having their creative efforts appreciated by others
- performing, observing & listening

and opportunities to –

- practise & refine skills & techniques
- express feelings, likes & dislikes
- develop their ideas

- select materials & tools for their tasks & projects
- explore colour & form
- listen to, respond (through speech & action) & appreciate music from a variety of cultures, genres & historical contexts
- share & appreciate others work
- make their own music
- see, hear & talk to musicians & artists
- retell stories through drama
- work in 2D & 3D
- explore sound, colour, texture, shape, form & space in 2 & 3 dimensions
- see, use, talk about a variety of voices & instruments
- see & talk about the work of other artists & art in the environment
- design, make & evaluate
- observe others using tools, media & equipment
- practise & improve their use of tools & techniques
- take part in a range of imaginative play situations
- take part in performances
- see that an aesthetic environment is important
- see the teacher as role model in role play, drawing, writing, dancing, imagining, etc.
- listen to, compose, appreciate music & to discuss likes & dislikes
- participate in displaying their own and others' work

Activities

- drawing with pencils, pens, crayons, felt tips, etc.
- painting with brushes of different sizes & types, sponges, fingers, feathers, sticks, combs, etc.
- printing with a variety of materials & natural & man made objects
- blowing, tipping, folding, pushing manipulating paint, paint rollers, sponge dabbers; marble rolling or ball rolling
- large scale painting – big brushes & paper; small scale painting – fine brushes, cotton buds, small paper
- a range of different painting techniques such as water-colour, dry paint on wet surface, comb painting; wax resist; leaf & other printing; splash, finger, foot painting; sponge, vegetable, shape, string prints; marbling, blot painting, blow painting, bubble printing, icing sugar
- painting on different surfaces – foil, card, newspaper, fabric, polystyrene, wallpaper, plaster, wood
- mixing paint, dry and wet, limiting colours and shades
- mixing things in the paint – glue, sand, rice, cornflour, sawdust
- group drawings & paintings with paper taped to table or floor
- different surfaces (table, easel, floor, outside) & sizes/shapes/types of paper
- decorating cakes
- PVA & tissue on black plastic, peel off when dry & cut into shapes for window decorations
- collage using a wide range of materials
- masks from paper bags & paper plates; hats
- pattern making with a variety of tools and media
- rubbings & etchings for texture, engrave polystyrene tiles with a pencil
- sketch books & observational drawing
- modelling with clay, papier mache, dough, pastry, etc.xture, shapes)

- collage with natural, found & waste materials (colour, tetearing, cutting, sticking, building)
- decoupage – cutting out pictures from magazines to make patterns, collage & 3D effects
- cooked & uncooked pasta with scissors
- model making with junk, clay, papier mache, dough, recycled materials
- making patterns, shapes, animals or people from clay, dough, salt dough, plasticene, cornflour, etc.
- copying rhythms, games with pauses, body music, telling stories with musical instruments
- ring games, songs & stories
- making, playing & listening to a variety of percussion & pitched instruments
- listening to a range of music from a range of artists & periods
- sound area with junk & sticks
- using their bodies in response to different stimuli
- experience art, music, dance, drama as a participant & a spectator
- experience a range of different musical & artistic styles
- observe others making music, moving & creating
- daily listening & responding to music
- music corner with home made instruments
- high/low notes on piano for movement
- listening walk (catch a sound in each hand, close fist when you have caught a sound)
- moving & making music to stories
- scarves or ribbons for movement; sensory/sound corner; tactile lotto; taste games; feely box
- taking photos, making tapes & video

Resources & equipment

- space to work
- range of paints in different colours, shades & textures (with sand, glue, flour)
- range of papers
- variety of brushes & other mark makers, felt pens, crayons, pencils.
- other tools for applying paint (e.g. sponges and rollers)
- materials for printing, collage & modelling
- pictures & prints from a range of artists, cultures & times
- materials & fabrics (natural & man made) for texture & colour
- substances to mix with paint & glue, peat, cornflour, sand, pasta, soapflakes, washing up liquid, sawdust
- play dough, dough with different flavouring, scent, texture and different qualities
- clay of different types and colours
- lacing cards & materials for sewing
- left & right handed scissors
- bank of cards & pictures
- posters, magazines & catalogues, calendar pictures & prints, photocopies to enlarge or reduce
- images, photos, recycled materials, sequins, glitter, feathers.
- large flat table/ floor/wall space
- shelving for storage, aprons
- easels
- plastic storage containers, small containers, spoons, knives
- plastic water containers, mixing palettes variety of prop boxes to change focus
- construction, waste, recycled, junk materials
- boards, tools, trays, rollers, pattern makers, dishes and pans, aprons
- cutters, rollers, knives, tools, flour and water to change texture

- tapes, records, pictures of musicians & instruments from a variety of cultures & times
- recordings of a wide range of music; tapes and player
- simple percussion instruments, pitched and not; home made instruments
- songbooks
- pencils and paper to write songs, and music
- role play with all purpose garments, lengths of material, shoes, cloaks
- bags, boxes, baskets, paper bags
- range of materials & equipment for dramatic & imaginative play
- collection of items other than instruments for making sounds (e.g. chimes, rattles, squeakers)
- sound makers, artefacts for dramatic play & acting out of stories
- musical instruments, bought & made
- cones, tubes, etc. to make instruments
- small world (e.g. Play People, Lego, puppets)
- dressing up clothes & lengths of fabric, hats & bags
- puppets
- face coloured pens, crayons, paint for a range of skin colours
- books & tapes for drama & movement
- dolls, farm, zoo, floor mats, railway
- cleaning cloths for children to use
- furniture (child and adult sized)
- real cooking implements in a range of sizes and from different cultures
- empty containers and bottles
- dolls, soft toys and clothes
- realistic ornaments
- books, magazines

5. Personal & social development

Outcomes at age 5 in knowledge, skills, understanding and attitudes

Early Learning Goals

* continue to be interested, excited and motivated to learn
* be confident to try new activities, initiate ideas and speak in a familiar group;
* maintain attention, concentration and sit quietly when appropriate;
* have a developing awareness of their own needs, views and feelings and be sensitive to the needs, views and feelings of others;
* have a developing respect for their own cultures and beliefs and those of other people;
* respond to significant experiences, showing a range of feelings when appropriate
* form good relationships with adults and peers;
* work as part of a group or class, taking turns and sharing fairly, understanding that there need to be agreed values, and codes of behaviour for groups of people, including adults and children, to work together harmoniously
* understand what is right, what is wrong and why;
* dress and undress independently and manage their own personal hygiene
* select and use activities and resources independently;
* consider the consequences of their words and actions for themselves and others;
* understand that people have different needs, views, cultures and beliefs, which need to be treated with respect;
* understand that they can expect others to treat their needs, views, cultures and beliefs with respect.

Additional Outcomes

* can work & play co-operatively & independently; is aware of own and others' safety
* can come into & go out of the classroom on their own
* can take responsibility for his/her own actions & the consequences of their behaviour
* can initiate new ideas, contribute to group times
* can talk about and control feelings, showing wonder, joy, interest, curiosity, sorrow, anger, frustration, etc., without losing control
* can communicate confidently with familiar adults & children
* shows kindness, sensitivity & respect for others, their cultures & beliefs
* shows sensitivity to the environment and is considerate to all living things
* is a good team member & understands winning & losing
* is confident & independent in familiar situations and is eager to learn
* knows & understands acceptable behaviour & simple rules of right & wrong
* knows that everyone is different, has feelings & that what we do may have an effect on others
* can choose activities and can take turns and share games, equipment and teacher/adult time
* can ask for help when needed
* knows that everyone in school has their best interests at heart
* has developed some self awareness, a sense of self worth & self esteem
* can make friends

Key experiences to build the above

Children should have opportunities to –

* experience being part of a group – take part in group activities in a variety of situations including free & structured play
* take part in discussions in groups of different sizes, to listen actively
* express & begin to control their feelings
* be involved in routines in school/nursery, learn to look after themselves & take appropriate responsibility to organise themselves & their belongings
* experience success
* go out into the local environment, & see plants, animals, etc.
* have contact with others of different ages, races, backgrounds & beliefs
* be in a safe, stable, happy, exciting environment where everyone is valued
* experience open questioning with enough time to reflect and respond
* experience & talk about the wonder of the world
* experience freedom to explore new situations, experiment & play
* recognise the feelings of others; 'put themselves in others' shoes' through discussion & role play
* take responsibility for their own actions and simple tasks
* experience quiet areas & reflective activities
* develop a sense of right & wrong
* communicate & work with peers & adults
* experience a secure world with clear & consistent rules & rewards
* discuss the results of their actions & make decisions over right & wrong
* make amends in an appropriate way; meet & find out about a wide range of people & events & respond to them
* experience new activities, people & learning experiences in & out of school/nursery

* experience information technology & other aids to learning
* recognise & appreciate abilities & disabilities
* involve their families in their learning
* be involved in the local community
* share, take turns, make choices, work alone, in pairs & groups
* concentrate & persevere in a task
* experience a range of feelings through stories & creative work, & to express these in appropriate ways
* appreciate the qualities of others & of themselves
* set & recognise the achievement of their own goals with appropriate adult support
* see good role models in the adults who work with them
* develop confidence, self help skills & independence
* look after living things, the environment & property
* experience the food, clothing, belongings & lifestyles of children from other backgrounds, faiths & cultures

- names on pegs, milk, name cards, group lists
- proper use of toilet, washing hands, blowing noses, etc.
- dressing & undressing in the home corner, PE, swimming, dressing for outside & going home
- socialising in dramatic play, discussion time, group work, games with rules
- circle, group & discussion times (with a shell or other object to pass to the speaker)
- looking after pets, visiting babies, parties & celebrations
- team and co-operative games such as parachutes games
- understanding drugs & medicines (through health projects)
- imaginative use of the classroom to simulate real life experiences (e.g. doctor's surgery, chip shop, travel agent, supermarket)
- opportunities to understand a range of cultures (e.g. celebrations, cooking)
- cooking, lunch & milk times, healthy eating projects
- paired work given a shared goal, such as a model to make together
- happy/sad book or poster
- target setting, work routines & achievement lists (e.g. an achievement wall or tree)
- personal profiles
- making & sharing food
- group collage, painting, construction – with group task
- activities to develop choice – materials & methods of working, partners, group members
- planning their own day or their own work

- wide range of visitors to talk & work with children (e.g. nurse, dentist, doctor, policeman)
- use TV, video, posters, photos to show & talk about other cultures & places
- taking messages, fetching things
- adults discussing learning with child, praise & reward to build confidence & self image
- involving parents, e.g. family group time in nursery
- drawing round each other
- sharing games, puzzles, painting, reading; using computer in pairs
- music & songs
- dressing dolls & teddies, tying laces, fastening buttons, zips, etc.
- ordering & sequencing songs games & activities
- shared & paired activities with older children (e.g. reading, music, stories)
- class assemblies
- sports & fun days
- getting out & putting away equipment & toys
- acting out stories, story time topics & themes, books containing stories with a moral, stories from different cultures
- road safety, health & related topics
- sharing toys, tidying up & putting away
- board games, ring games, group activities

Resources & equipment

- sensitive & knowledgeable adult support
- child-size coat pegs, toilets & washbasins
- stories which contain or illustrate social, moral, spiritual and cultural themes
- stories, pictures, labels, notices, posters & artefacts reflecting a range of cultures and in a range of languages/scripts
- equipment to promote personal care, organisation, responsibility (e.g. dressing, shoelace tying)
- looking after themselves & others
- puppets & small world people
- jigsaws, board games, dice, card games from a wide range of cultures
- books of children's games including those for the outside

- clothes & dolls clothes from a range of cultures
- role play areas & appropriate equipment
- dressing up clothes
- food & cooking utensils from other countries and cultures
- resource list of local places of interest to visit
- living things to care for (e.g. plants, bulbs, seeds)
- parachute & book of games
- recipe books
- photos of families to discuss
- good storage and access

6. Physical development

Outcomes at age 5 in knowledge, skills, understanding and attitudes

Early Learning Goals

* move with confidence, imagination and in safety;
* move with control and co-ordination;
* show awareness of space, of themselves and others;
* recognise the importance of keeping healthy and those things which contribute to this;
* recognise the changes that happen to their bodies when they are active;
* use a range of small and large equipment;
* travel around, under, over & through balancing and climbing equipment;
* handle tools, objects, construction and malleable materials safely and with increasing control.

Additional Outcomes

* knows the main parts of the body & how the body works
* knows how equipment works
* knows some vocabulary of movement (hop, skip, jump, etc.)
* understands aspects of movement such as speed. shape, space
* knows how to control his/her body in different situations
* realises s/he has responsibility for clearing up
* can use a range of tools & can select the right tool for the job
* can control large toys
* has respect for others' space & activities
* is able to line up, take turns, space out, find a space, move without bumping into others

(Outcomes — continued)

* can perform individually, in pairs & small groups to a familiar audience
* can use tools, construction & malleable materials with increasing control
* can get out, use & put away simple large & small apparatus
* can handle objects with care & control
* knows & understands the reasons for & can follow simple rules for PE
* can balance & climb with reasonable agility & skill on a range of large & small apparatus
* can throw, catch, balance, skip, hop, climb, ride a bike/trike
* can use scissors, writing implements, pegboards, etc.
* can thread, build, manipulate small objects
* can design, make & talk about structures, models & other artefacts
* is agile, flexible, controlled, confident, enthusiastic & able to work safely
* is confident & co-ordinated using both gross & fine motor skills
* responds to a range of stimuli, sounds, music & voices, & enjoys physical activity
* is aware of space & others when moving & using apparatus & tools

Key experiences to build the above

Children should have access to –

* a range of well maintained & appropriate large & small equipment & apparatus, a range of surfaces & spaces both indoors & out
* a range of tools & materials
* activities, materials & equipment for fixing, screwing, cutting, threading, folding, bending, shaping, indoor & outdoor play, structured & child initiated
* malleable & other materials – clay, dough, plasticene sand, paint, water, wood, glue
* puppets, finger play & rhymes, ring games & songs
* group activities such as parachutes, team games, paired games
* a safe, well supervised physical environment which offers a range of new and structured challenges
* activities which develop control, co-ordination, confidence, promoting a healthy lifestyle

and opportunities to –

* move on different surfaces and explore what their bodies can do
* talk about the body, develop personal hygiene
* understand the importance of fresh air, exercise & a healthy diet

(Key experiences — continued)

* develop a sense of safety & appropriate use of tools & apparatus
* see, explore & develop physical skills (e.g. balancing, climbing, running, catching, throwing)
* design & make large & small models & structures with a variety of materials
* change their environment by their own efforts, using tools, equipment, discussion
* see good models of adults & other children using apparatus & equipment
* move in a variety of ways & spaces: move to music, dance & make music
* talk about equipment & movement; plan sequences of movement, using equipment
* cut, stick, cook, trace, colour, paint, thread; fasten buttons & zips, tie laces; use instruments, computer keyboard, tapes & telephones
* adapt things for a new purpose
* work in pairs & groups, practise skills in play situations
* develop spatial awareness & the language that goes with it
* move in different ways alone, with large & small apparatus & wheeled toys
* use a range of construction toys & apparatus which encourages development of fine motor skills, hand/eye co-ordination & fine motor control

- bubble blowing, jigsaws, bricks, floor puzzles, puppets, games, model making
- threading & threading patterns such as sewing cards from Christmas cards
- dressing and undressing, washing, use of cutlery
- hand & finger games
- construction toys which encourage connection, disconnection, balance, control, stacking, building
- bridges & tunnels for small toys & play people
- sewing, sticking, binding, wrapping, folding, cutting, shaping, tearing
- woodwork, clay, dough, sand, water
- pouring, tipping, filling, emptying
- cooking, chopping, stirring, mixing, serving, laying table, washing up, putting things away
- outside play, swimming & more formal PE
- simple games & activities of throwing & catching, jumping, running, rolling, balancing, crawling, climbing, skipping, hopping, sliding
- small group games, team games, ring games, body games
- imaginative movement, with or without music
- drama, 'lets pretend'
- making tents & camps, dens making maps & plans, treasure hunts & trails
- PE activities - dodging, travelling, balancing: indoor PE activities with small apparatus
- games to involve positional & spatial vocabulary – behind, under, over, through; & patterns of movement
- 'I can' games

- songs, rhymes & games to encourage body control & language, Simon Says, Grandmother's Footsteps, catch, put your finger in the air, follow the leader, etc.
- team challenges (e.g. Lets All Pull Together)
- tug of war
- mazes, challenges, obstacle races
- chalk games on playground – snakes, hopscotch, footsteps, lines
- free & structured activities for warming up
- playing, responding to & listening to percussion instruments & other music
- simple rhythm & pattern on instruments
- riding bikes, trikes, scooters, trolleys – pulling, pushing, steering
- parachute & other co-operative games
- sponge ball chase
- tail catch with a band or ribbon in waistband
- traffic lights (walk, stop, sit, etc.)
- make tracks & paths with boards, planks, ropes, tunnels, hoops (or chalk on playground)
- Hot Rice, Ship to Shore
- opportunities for relaxation and meditation
- balancing an object on head, arm, back, etc.
- bats and balls, aiming at a target, into a container, through a goal or tunnel
- making gardens, digging holes

- free things from the real world – milk crates, plastic bottles, carpet samples, wooden & cardboard boxes, tubes from carpets, shavings
- cones, skittles, mats, quoits, bean bags, balancing boards
- sheets for tents & picnics
- wigs, hats, masks, picnic sets
- cement mixing trays
- scissors, rulers, magnets
- jigsaws, bricks, floor puzzles
- puppets, games
- posters & pictures of healthy food, parts of the body
- well maintained suitable large & small equipment for outdoor & indoor play & PE
- musical instruments
- tapes & records
- beads for threading, small objects for counting & sorting
- props & costumes for dramatic & imaginative play
- trampolines
- permanent & temporary markings on playgrounds and other surfaces (lines, targets, stepping stones, mazes, road markings, concentric circles, spirals, hopscotches, etc.)

- balancing beams, planks, cubes & tunnels
- climbing frames & slides, tyres, boxes, cardboard tubes, unit blocks
- large building blocks, planks, play cubes, solid steps
- large diameter tubes, cardboard boxes
- rope and string, small car tyres
- literacy materials (e.g. clipboard to encourage writing in creative & outdoor activities)
- large varied climbing structures with different attachments (e.g. poles, swings, ropes & ladders)
- barrels, pipes and stiles, fixed & free tyres, boats, engines, etc.
- trees, tree houses, tree stumps, rope frames, swings & slides
- indoor apparatus & mats
- soft play pieces
- games apparatus (e.g. bean bags, quoits, hoops, ropes, skittles, bats, balls)
- trikes, scooters, wheelbarrows, prams

Chapter 3

Writing a policy for the Early Years

'In our view, each institution should have ... a policy outlining aims and objectives, based on a clearly articulated philosophy shared by educators and parents.'

Starting with Quality, The Rumbold Committee, HMSO 1990

The curriculum for the Foundation Stage is an intentional curriculum. The activities which children follow, the experiences they have and the learning which comes from them should not be matters of chance. They should be intended and planned. We have suggested in earlier pages what the elements of such a curriculum should be, but that is only part of the story. An intentional curriculum must be defined. So that everyone involved can understand it, it is important for the definition to be expressed in a document. This will probably take the form of a statement of policy and principles, which may either stand alone as an expression of the principles and approach taken by a setting, or may be included as the first stage in a whole school curriculum policy statement.

The Rumbold Committee outlined the components of such a policy, and many schools have found this a helpful starting point. The Committee recommended that the policy should include –

- aims and objectives based on a clearly articulated philosophy such as –
   an atmosphere in which every child and adult feels secure, valued and confident
   a broad, balanced and relevant curriculum, appropriate to the social, emotional, spiritual and intellectual development of individual children, including those with special educational needs
   an approach to learning geared to the needs of young children, emphasising first hand experiences, play and talk, which is built on contributions from parent, educator and child, and which feeds and supports children's learning
- a statement about equal opportunities
- a statement about partnership with parents which acknowledges their role as children's prime educators
- details of liaison with other institutions
- arrangements for quality control, monitoring, evaluation and revision of policies, procedures and practice
- management structures
- planning assessment and record keeping for children in all areas of development
- staff development, training and experience of staff
- the ratio of educators to children
- support for a physical environment organised with due regard to health and safety, to meet the needs of young children, with appropriate space, facilities and equipment

The framework for an Early Years policy which follows is based on a series of questions. Answering these will enable the user to reflect on the above and express their views about each. Discussion at each stage will help to ensure that the policy has the support of all interested parties and can effectively guide the setting in managing its provision. A diagrammatic outline is followed by the detailed description of each

First Hand – auditing the curriculum for the under fives, and the accompanying computer disc take you step by step through the process of writing a policy for the Early Years.

Both are available from the publisher.

First Hand - making the Foundation Curriculum work

section. The Bibliography contains references to additional materials, research and the statutory background which will help you in your discussions. The companion publication, *First Hand – auditing the curriculum for the Early Years*, and the accompanying computer disc take you step by step through the process of writing a policy tailored to your own situation. There is nothing sacred about the suggested order of sections in the pages which follow, but we have found this to be an arrangement that works well.

**A Suggested Framework
for Curriculum
Documentation**

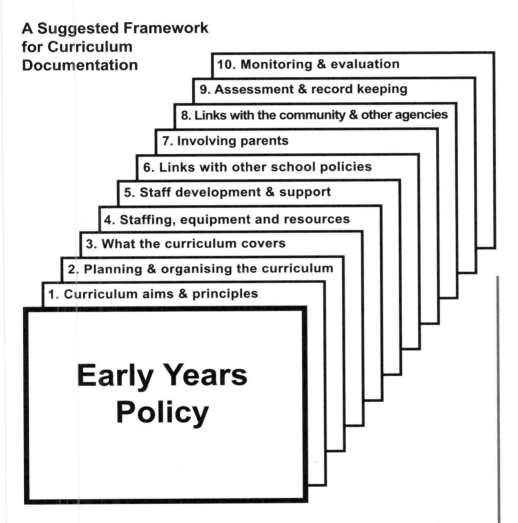

10. Monitoring & evaluation
9. Assessment & record keeping
8. Links with the community & other agencies
7. Involving parents
6. Links with other school policies
5. Staff development & support
4. Staffing, equipment and resources
3. What the curriculum covers
2. Planning & organising the curriculum
1. Curriculum aims & principles

**Early Years
Policy**

Why is the Early Years curriculum different and important?

Your policy and practice in the Early Years should be guided by clear principles, and you need to say at the outset what these are. You may already have a set of agreed aims and principles by which you work. If not, you may wish to use the ones we suggest in Chapter 1, adopt or adapt a statement from one of the documents we list in the bibliography, or base them on those from another setting. *A Curriculum for the Pre-school Child* (Audrey M. Curtis, NFER-Nelson, 1986) and *Starting*

**Policy Section 1
Curriculum
aims and
principles**

with Quality are particularly useful sources. You may also decide to include some of the wording from the Guidance for the Foundation Stage. Whichever you choose, the principles ought, of course, to reinforce and expand your own aims. They should be discussed by and agreed with all staff. In the case of a school, the policy will also need to have the approval of the governing or managing body. In all settings the support of parents and other stakeholders is essential.

Policy Section 2 Planning and organising the curriculum

Section 2 - How is the provision organised and planned? The setting, its organisation and processes of teaching and learning.

How do you put the principles into practice? There should be a section covering organisational and practical issues, which might include short statements on whichever of the following are appropriate to your situation.

- admission, induction and entry arrangements, including the age of admission and transfer
- part and full time places, hours, etc.
- the structure of the day, starting and finishing times, breaks
- snack and lunchtime arrangements
- the organisation into classes or groups, including supervision
- location of the classes or groups within the building
- some idea of how children are grouped for different activities
- the place of outdoor play
- opportunities for joint activities with the whole school and with other classes
- information for parents and communication systems such as newsletters and meetings
- parents' role in supporting the school with a range of ideas
- reporting to parents on progress, parents evenings, etc.
- emergency contacts, allergies, accidents, what to do if a child is ill
- trips and visits

Policy Section 3 What the curriculum covers

Section 3 - What will the children be learning and when? How is the curriculum organised? What is the progression of teaching and learning?

A clear, concise explanation of how the curriculum for the Early Years is planned and organised should address the importance of play, talk and first hand experience. It should make clear how the curriculum is arranged (for example, whether activities are grouped within themes or otherwise organised), the sequence of activities and experiences, and how you use the Stepping Stones to ensure progress towards the *Early Learning Goals* and the National Curriculum for Key Stage 1.

We recommend that you include a curriculum map, as this will show the programme of study. You may wish to base it on the *First Hand curriculum map* we provide in Chapter 2, which can be adapted for a range of uses, or you may prefer to construct your own. If you work across a wide age range, you may want to add information to explain how progression is assured.

Section 4 - Who is involved and what is available for them to work with? Resources, including staffing, outside agencies, materials and equipment.

Staffing

In stating how the setting and its constituent groups are staffed, you should explain the different roles of everyone who contributes to the work of the setting - practitioners (including teachers, care assistants, nursery nurses and classroom support staff), students, volunteers and others. Guidance on managing and using parents and other resources from outside is given in Chapters 6 and 7.

When listing staff it is useful to include names, responsibilities, areas of special interest or expertise, and training. Job descriptions, or examples of these, could be included as appendices. Staff ratios, group sizes and other details of organisational structures also fit here.

If you are in a school you may also wish to include information about the school's access to expertise outside the Early Years department – for example, curriculum leaders and the SENCO (Special Educational Needs Co-ordinator). You could also clarify the roles and responsibilities of governors, management committees and senior managers.

Resources

Here you should make clear what resources are available to staff and children. You should include resources inside and outside the building – for example, play areas, outside toys and equipment, base room, hall, library, swimming pool, TV room and so on. You also need to locate the storage of materials for practitioners– consumables, teachers' books, teaching programmes, as well as those resources shared with other departments or settings, such as large apparatus, outside play facilities and equipment, music books, maths equipment and computer software. You may find it helpful to include a plan of the setting showing where these resources are located.

Budget

The mention of budgets often frightens people! All that needs to be said about the budget in the policy document is a short statement describing briefly the processes by which the budget is managed, and how decisions on needs and spending are made. It should make clear how priorities for the allocation of funds are established, and the way that emerging issues are resourced through normal planning routines and the creation of the setting's plan for development, management or improvement.

It is helpful to cover the provision of additional finance. This can include fund raising, finance from the parents, arrangements for handling petty cash and access to the school fund, and the policy on charging for activities could also be mentioned, as they apply in your situation.

Policy Section 5
Staff development and support

Section 5 - How do we improve our teaching skills and knowledge of how children learn?

The management of the setting will need some way of making sure that employees have the opportunity to refresh and develop their skills. The organisation of appraisal or professional development discussions may be the same throughout the setting, so reference could be made here to a staff handbook, staff development plan or other professional documents, if you have them. Staff development should include *all* staff, and ideally should also cover training for volunteers and students. There is guidance and information on this area in Chapter 6.

You may also wish to provide some information about the arrangements for meetings, planning sessions, training days, etc.

The induction and support of newly qualified and newly appointed staff would also fit in this section.

Policy Section 6
Links with other school policies

Section 6 - How does this policy link with other policies and statements?

If you are in a school you may well have whole school policies for most of the key areas listed below. In this case there is probably no need to write completely new and separate policies for the Early Years. It may be enough for your Early Years policy either to refer to existing documents or to include parts of them. In some cases you may want to write an additional paragraph or two in order to clarify their relevance to the Early Years. In any case it will be useful to include in your Early Years policy a list of whole school policy documents and where they can be found. If you are not in a school, your setting may well have statements about health and safety, accidents and emergencies, equal opportunities and so on which have been produced for guidance and support.

The essence of any policy is that it should clarify, guide and regulate practice. It is not unusual for practitioners, in preparing for inspection for example, to spend many hours writing over-lengthy policies which do not relate closely enough to what people actually do and think they should do. If you do not have policies in some of the areas suggested below we recommend that the best starting point is to write a very simple description of what you do, and to get a colleague or two to check it and confirm that it is what they do, too.

Links to other policies might make reference to -

- Health and safety
- Admissions
- Special needs
- Behaviour and discipline
- Assessments, records and reports
- Equal opportunities
- Charges for activities
- Complaints procedures

- Teaching and learning
- Child protection
- Support for children who have English as an additional language (EAL)

Section 7 - How are parents involved in the Early Years curriculum? How do they have access to the activities and to reports on their children's progress?

One of your principles will certainly be concerned with the role of parents in the education and care of their children. This section gives you the opportunity to identify the ways you put this into practice. Don't forget to include –

- parent consultations and advice (formal and informal)
- reports
- records and assessments, including parents' role in the baseline assessment of children
- book and toy libraries
- parenting classes and other training
- support for bi-lingual families and those who do not speak English
- support and advice for the parents of children with special needs
- parent help in your activities
- parent associations
- social and fund raising activities
- parental involvement in home activities, for example shared reading
- support and links with other agencies such as health, social services, special needs

Section 8 - How do we involve other agencies, support services and the local community?

Your policy for the Early Years will benefit from a short section on the way you keep in touch with and use support services and resources outside the school or nursery. Think about such services as –

- school health and health visiting
- speech therapy
- education welfare and social services
- paediatric and other hospital outreach
- community centres and local support workers, including faith groups
- the school psychological service
- local groups for family support
- bilingual, and other EAL teams
- other local schools, playgroups and nurseries

Chapter 7 will help you with this section.

Section 9 - How do we know how well the children are doing?

This section covers the whole area of baseline assessment, recording progress, reports, records of achievement, moderation, portfolios,

**Policy Section 7
Involving parents**

**Policy Section 8
Links with the
community &
other agencies**

**Policy Section 9
Assessment &
record keeping**

target setting, etc. It should cover all assessment, recording and reporting procedures, from pre-admission information to transfer to Key Stage 1. You should include details of the arrangements for liaison with previous and future educational settings, either within the school or with other organisations in the community.

What you say here will mirror, or may already be contained in, your assessment, recording and reporting policy. Consider providing brief information on each of the topics in the list below. Be sure to say when the various assessment activities take place, where this is relevant.

- entry profiles and baseline assessments
- observations and record keeping
- self assessment ('I can') information
- contributions from parents
- diagnostic and attainment tests, if or when used
- records of achievement
- target setting
- reports to parents
- transfer information from pre-school settings and to other classes, groups and schools

Include blank examples of your paperwork (baseline assessments, records, reports and target setting documents, etc.), so that everyone can recognise them and be clear about their purpose.

Policy Section 10 Monitoring & evaluation

Section 10 - How do we know how well the curriculum is working?

It is important to monitor your policy in action, and to set up arrangements for its regular review. Therefore a section on monitoring and evaluation should be part of any curriculum document. Chapter 8 contains a review of methods of monitoring and evaluating what you do, and suggests the advantages and disadvantages of each. It will help you with this section of your policy.

We suggest you include information on some or all of the following –

- observation by practitioners themselves
- observation and other ways of monitoring by others, including inspection (remember to refer back to the significant findings of previous inspections)
- evaluation of the curriculum, analysis of statistical information, reviews of targets and staff discussions
- the use of LEA and other external monitoring and advice

We suggest that you take a good look at your policy each year. Doing this takes some discipline, and we recommend that at the beginning of the year you fix when this is to be done and set aside some time for it.

At its simplest the purpose of this review is to check that you have not forgotten what you said when you wrote the policy in the first place! Practice sometimes drifts under the pressure of everyday work, and it is surprising how easily this can happen. More importantly, however, it

First Hand - making the Foundation Curriculum work

will help you to ensure that the policy is still relevant to the needs of your situation, and that it is being followed by everyone involved. Exactly how you carry out this review needs some thought, but key features will be a re-reading of the policy document, observation of how staff apply elements of the policy during their daily work, and discussion with members of staff. Chapter 8 will give you some ideas.

Barring major changes in the organisation of your setting or demands created by new national requirements, this annual monitoring will not normally result in a major overhaul of the contents of the policy. It is, rather, a refreshing and updating.

We recommend that you carry out a full review and, if necessary, revision of the policy every three or four years, although it may be triggered sooner by significant changes in circumstances within the Early Years context. Of course, your policy will only be effective if all staff know it, understand it and support it in practice.

Readers will need to know when the policy was produced, so don't forget to date it, sign it, and set a date for review.

Summary

- Every establishment catering for under fives should have a written document expressing its curriculum policy.
- The document should underpin practice in all areas of the provision.
- The policy should reflect the aims and principles of the school/setting.
- It should be cross referenced to and supported by other policies, where relevant.
- The written policy should be monitored regularly, to ensure that it informs and reflects practice
- It should be available to, and be supported by, all stakeholders.

Formal & informal assessment

Planning and organising an appropriate curriculum requires sensitivity to the needs of each child in the group, while retaining the principle that there is a common core of experiences which is the right of each of those children – the entitlement curriculum. There is also the responsibility to ensure that an organised Early Years setting offers enhancements which go beyond what the child would probably have experienced if he or she remained exclusively within the home environment for the same period.

However, the notion of an entitlement which meets the needs of the individual child is mere rhetoric if we fail to take into full account not only the age of the child, but also his or her stage of development on entry to the formal Early Years setting. How else can we find the right place to start? Accurate baseline information is essential. It is the bedrock on which the child's experience of the curriculum is built and developed, the first identification of present needs and future potential.

Baseline assessments should be made as soon as possible after the child has entered the group. However, starting school, nursery or kindergarten is a new experience. The mere fact of being in an unfamiliar environment may cause the child to display behaviour outside his or her normal pattern. This may distort attempts to assess what he or she knows, understands and can do, and result in inaccurate or incomplete data. Because of this some practitioners choose to defer baseline assessment until they are sure that the child has settled. However, if the baseline is to convey an accurate picture of the child at the beginning of his or her time with us, we must not leave baseline assessments so late that the information is no longer a true baseline at all.

Practitioners make many assessments of children before, during and after entry to school. Some of these are formal – screenings, question-naires, structured and recorded observations, home visits, discussions with parents and carers and booklets with activities for parents and children. Some of them are informal and usually rest on observation – for example, behaviour in the group and with parents, discussions and demonstrations, objects made, games played, interactions with others. Many of these informal assessments remain in the practitioners head and are unrecorded except in brief notes and reminders. For the most part they are part of the vast store of data that exists in the practitioners' own minds.

Together these two types of assessment enable us to build up a complex picture of the whole child as he or she enters this first period of formal education. If they are sensitively used they can form the basis for a curriculum which starts where the child is and builds on what he or she has already learned. This is the central purpose of baseline assessment and the most important use of the information gathered – to ensure that the activities and experiences offered are matched as closely as possible to the needs of the individual child.

Of course, this is not the only purpose of baseline assessment. The national focus on raising standards and improving provision relies on the collection and aggregation of information about attainment. In some cases such information is used to make crude comparisons between children, schools and organisations, ignoring their individuality and the contexts in which they live and learn. The result is 'league tables', which on the whole do little more than compare attainment at the end of a period of schooling, without any recognition or acknowledgement of how much progress has been made. There is now a growing understanding that measuring 'added value' through benchmarking, and the inclusion of a wider range of information, give a better indication of the real improvement and progress of individuals and groups.

Baseline information is needed for two quite separate purposes. Strategic decision making at all levels, from the current development or management plan to government initiatives and targeted funding, requires whole cohort, setting or school, and national information. However, this strategic element is only half the picture. Accurate baseline information is the starting point for teachers and others in planning a curriculum which will meet individual needs.

So we have different purposes for the collection of information – that which benefits the child as an individual and that which is needed for measuring the effectiveness of provision as a whole. Practitioners should ask the following questions before collecting any information about children –

- Why are we collecting this information?
- Who will use it, and how?
- Is this the most effective, manageable and appropriate way of collecting the information?
- Who will have access to the information collected?
- Is this assessment and all that it involves in the best interests of the child?

In the rest of this chapter we have tried to clarify the different types of information currently collected, to identify the purposes and uses of each, and to outline briefly the chief features of current practice.

The purposes of baseline assessment fall into four categories – national, LEA, school or setting, and individual. Each needs different types of data and detail of information, and each supports a different level of strategic planning.

National baseline data, collected through national baseline assessments, informs government by providing statistics on a large scale for public reports, league tables and reviews of standards. This data is used in establishing policy at the macro level and in interpreting that policy at a local level. It enables policy makers to gain a national overview and contributes to the background against which large scale initiatives are developed. Sometimes it has an effect on the ability of

value added –
an assessment of progress which an individual or school makes between points of measurement – e.g. the progress made by a child between entry to school and the age of 7 or 11

benchmarking –
an assessment of progress or attainment compared with a group of other schools or settings with like features, such as the percentage of free school meals, or children with English as an additional language

National baselines

- that the most reliable information is collected through **observation** during appropriate activities in familiar settings
- that **timing** is important – information can be collected before entry, but if the assessment is to give a true baseline it should be carried out as near to the point of entry as possible
- that the process should be **manageable** in scope and in its requirements for time and paperwork.

Summary

- The most important function of baseline assessment is to inform teacher planning and to ensure that the curriculum meets the needs of the child.
- Baseline assessment is a complex and vital activity.
- Information gathered is used for a range of purposes, and we should be aware of those purposes before embarking on the assessment.
- Assessment provides information for strategic and operational planning.
- National baseline assessment requirements on their own do not provide enough information for planning the curriculum.

This example of baseline screening has been developed at Coleman Primary School, Leicester. The school has a high proportion of children with English as an additional language and many children entering the school speak no English at all, so it is important for the school to judge the language level of entrants. Nursery and Reception staff used a combination of sources and based the screening on the Desirable Outcomes, *so that the child's progress towards these can be measured.*

Practitioners are now checking such screenings with the Stepping Stones to ensure a good match and coverage of the strands within the areas of learning. As the single national baseline is introduced, it would also be advisable to check that the selection of stepping stones in a 3 or 4 year old screening include the goals covered by the national assessment at the end of reception. In this way, it would be possible to calculate the value added during the Foundation Stage.

Personal & Social Development	Language & Literacy (in MT & English)		Mathematics	Knowledge & Understanding of the World	
• happy to come to school • confident to leave parents • interacts with adults & other children • chooses & engages in an activity • can share toys • can work/play on his/her own • states needs	• communicates with peers • communicates with adults • communicates willingly/happily • can follow simple instruction • listens to stories • shows interest in books • understands how books work • joins in and enjoys songs/rhymes • responds to name • has clear speech		• can chant numbers • can count to 2/5/10 and beyond • can recognise/name some colours • can sort (e.g. colour or shape) • knows/can name some simple shapes • uses some mathematical language (e.g. big/small) • can recognise some numbers	• can find their way about the nursery • talks about experiences in and out of school • is willing to explore new equipment and activities • asks questions • can describe things	
Physical Development	Self help & Independence		Creative Development	KEY	
• can hold/use pencil/crayon to make a mark • can move with confidence and control (inc. steps) • can pedal a tricycle • can do a simple inset puzzle • can build a tower of 5 bricks • can thread beads	• can sit & look at a book • can use toilet independently • joins in group activities • responds to simple instructions • can fetch and put on their coat • can choose an activity • is willing to leave parent/carer without undue distress		• enjoys creative activities • involves him/herself in imaginative play • enjoys playing with natural materials (sand, water, play dough) • attempts to be creative with construction toys • enjoys painting activities	/ Poor ∟ Fair △ Good △ A real strength ? Possible problems	

Reproduced by kind permision of Coleman Primary School, Leicester

RVNIL

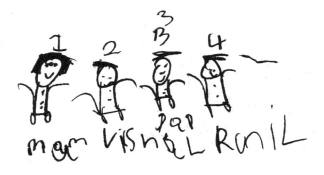

mam VISNEL RCNIL

Chapter 5

Deciding what to do next
(Planning)

We have argued in preceding chapters that the Early Years curriculum is intentional, and therefore needs to be planned. In this chapter we explore some of the issues connected with planning and provide some examples which readers may wish to adopt for their own uses.

Planning is essentially a practical activity, which should lead to practical outcomes. It must be informative without being too time consuming. If it is to be efficient and effective it should be a collaborative process, preferably involving all those who will have a part in implementing the plan. There are three layers to planning – long term planning, which identifies **what** we should teach; medium term planning, which identifies **when** we should teach, and short term planning, which identifies **how** we should teach. This way of breaking down a whole curriculum ensures both coverage and manageability.

Long term planning – *what* we should teach

The long term plan is the map of the experiences which will be offered to children during the Early Years. It relates to the aims of the setting and incorporates national requirements and guidance. It establishes the major objectives and outcomes for teaching and learning and prepares children to embark on the National Curriculum at Key Stage 1. These outcomes are assessed at the time of the baseline assessment which is carried out as children begin their statutory education at the end of Reception. Long term planning should recognise both the circumstances of the individual school, and the national context and advice as contained in the Foundation Guidance and the National Curriculum.

Medium term planning – *when* we should teach

Medium term planning is about when we should teach the elements of the long term plan. The long term plan, however detailed and helpful, does not in itself provide a manageable model for practical work in the setting. Medium term planning breaks down the long term plan into workable units, taking a group of major learning intentions and setting out over a few weeks or half a term the experiences intended to achieve them. In most groups, medium term planning consists of thematic elements (topics, themes or key questions) and core elements (work on developing children's grasp of such key skills as literacy, numeracy, physical or motor skills, personal and social development and under-standing of the world around them). Medium term planning also addresses the balance between teaching and assessment.

Short term planning – *how* we should teach

At this stage we take the medium term plan and from it identify short term intentions, which we can translate into a flexible range of activities for the day or the week. Short term plans deal with organisation, grouping, differentiation and support from staff, materials and equipment. They also provide a framework for ongoing assessment and allow adjustment from day to day so that we can ensure that the activities are meeting the developing needs of the children.

Planning	Assessment	Evaluation
LONG TERM (e.g. a year)		
CONTENT 　areas of learning 　all learning outcomes - skills, 　　concepts, knowledge, 　　attitudes	baselines for whole setting assessment	cyclical annual whole school contribution to 　evaluation of whole plan, 　especially core skills
MEDIUM TERM **(e.g. half a term)**		
CONTENT 　areas of learning 　selected learning outcomes 　selected examples of good 　　practice 　• learning - skills, 　　concepts, knowledge, 　　attitudes 　• activities 　• assessment	baselines for a cohort at a time group targets formative assessment for cohorts and groups	annual evaluation of coverage end of topic adjustment of 　coverage
SHORT TERM **(e.g. a day or week)** (detailed learning programme for individual and groups of children, specific to their current needs i.e. adult-directed + child initiated experiences)		
CONTENT 　devised from medium term 　　planning 　areas of learning/specific 　　learning outcomes 　specific examples of good 　　practice 　• learning - skills, con- 　　cepts, knowledge, 　　attitudes 　• activities - organisa- 　　tion, resources, differen- 　　tiation	baselines for individuals and groups individual and group targets assessment through 　observation - activities 　and outcomes	daily/weekly notes to inform medium and long term evaluations

The 'map' included in Chapter 2 provides a basis for long term planning.
See Example 1 at the end of this Chapter for a suggested framework.

The detail of layered planning

In effective planning, the three different 'layers' (long, medium and short term) are clear. Some agreement exists across the setting of the processes and the documentation, the documents (at least at long and medium term) are public, and the planning recognises both the 'thematic or topic' curriculum and the ongoing or basic curriculum.

The needs of young children require a flexible approach to planning, which gives scope for modification in response to individuals and groups. However, flexibility must support the intended curriculum rather than drive it. Regular review will ensure that breadth and balance are maintained.

Curriculum maps (long term)

Teachers need to establish a 'map' of the experiences they intend to offer to children during their time in the Foundation groups and classes. It is easier when these are grouped using some sort of structure such as the six areas of learning ndescribed in the QCA Guidance. Practitioners can then decide which range of themes across a year (or even a term) will offer the best coverage of the 'map', ensuring the development of essential knowledge, skills understanding and attitudes.

Themes and modules (medium term)

Schools often employ a series of loose theme titles which give the best coverage of the map over a period of usually of a year, or sometimes two. Using the themes as guidance, teachers are able to draw up a half termly plan which identifies the activities through which the experiences covered in the long term plan will be provided, and locates key major objectives for the planning period. It is unlikely that the planned theme will include the whole range of experiences in the long term plan. Teachers need to decide just what the theme offers, and whether they will need to supplement it with other things.

Balancing the core and thematic elements – see examples 2 & 3 at the end of this Chapter.

In many settings the thematic elements are planned in more detail and recorded more thoroughly than the core or ongoing elements. Core skills activities (e.g. sand, water, imaginative play, books, outside play, etc.) should be planned with just as much care and attention, as these form the basis for much of the curriculum for children under five, and pratically those under three (See example 6). Practitioners should look carefully at the balance of emphasis, the time spent and the value given to these two elements of the medium term plan. Themes should be seen not as ends in themselves but as vehicles for exciting and relevant practice and the development of core skills through 'real life' situations and practical activities.

Many practitioners also have a map of core skills and ongoing experiences. These are often planned in blocks or rotations so that they can be both differentiated according to the needs of the children, and revisited at regular intervals to provide a broad range of activities, supporting specific skills.

A useful – and portable! – checklist for remembering the core elements and the six areas of experience is to think of them as related to the fingers of both hands.

The core elements & the areas of experience

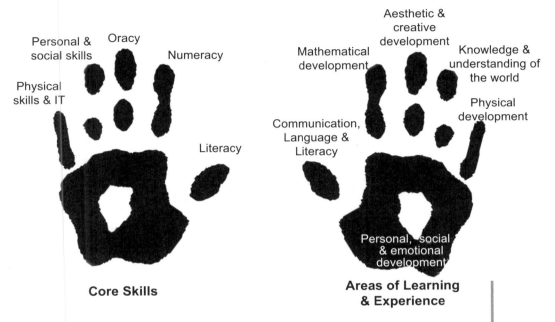

Personal & social skills
Oracy
Numeracy
Physical skills & IT
Literacy

Core Skills

Aesthetic & creative development
Mathematical development
Knowledge & understanding of the world
Physical development
Communication, Language & Literacy
Personal, social & emotional development

Areas of Learning & Experience

The week and the day (short term)

Using the themes and their associated core activities, practitioners draw up weekly and daily plans which address the objectives in detail and identify groupings and resources. Weekly and daily plans should state a manageable number of short term intentions which relate directly to those in the medium term plan.

Efficient practitioners will identify key objectives for whole sessions, days and weeks (even right across the group/class). This helps them to choose activities and equipment which ensure that priorities are met and progress is recognised and recorded. Short term planning should take account of the needs of individuals and groups, either in order to meet special needs or to ensure that special skills, interests and aptitudes are acknowledged. Practitioners often remark that finding enough time for such planning is a problem. However, good planning can *save* time. If the content of the short term plan is both manageable and clear, teachers will be able to build in the time and the focus for observation and assessment because they will not have to spend as much time on unscheduled and purely reactive activity, while still ensuring flexibility.

Observation, assessment and regular monitoring of the curriculum in action are essential elements of good teaching. They also assist with the review of medium and long term planning, ensuring that the long

The key questions for planning are reproduced with acknowledgements to Joan Dean, 'Organising Learning in the Primary School'.

term objectives in the curriculum plan are met.

Whether you are basing your teaching on a topic or responding more flexibly to children's interests and emerging needs with a discrete subject, the following key questions will help you in your planning –

1. What have the children already experienced?
   (**baseline information** about what children already know and can do, located in the Stepping Stones)
2. How can I plan to offer practical learning experiences so that the children fully understand what they are doing?
   (planning **'first hand' experiences**)
3. What are the influences of language and vocabulary on learning? How do I balance present language levels, the need for language practice and reinforcement, and the introduction of new vocabulary and language?
   (planning for **communication and language development**)
4. What do I hope children will know and understand at the end of this piece of work?
   (**knowledge and concept objectives**)
5. What do I hope that the children will be able to do as a result of this piece of work?
   (**skills objectives**)
6. How will I know what they have learnt?
   (observing and assessing the **learning outcomes**)
7. How do I ensure that the children have a broad, balanced experience while recognising the value of child initiated activities and free play?
   (balancing **choice and direction**)
8. How can I use the outcomes of assessment in the next cycle of planning?
   (**monitoring and evaluation**)

The main purpose of planning is to ensure the continuity of children's learning and their smooth progression through the curriculum. Planning should, therefore, be a whole setting activity. The long term plan should form part of the whole learning map and should be shared with and understood by everyone who works in the setting, not just those who are involved with the Early Years. Medium and short term plans will probably vary in format and organisation in different parts of a school. However, they should be understood by everyone and should follow agreed principles. Planning at all levels and for all ages should identify clear objectives, ensure the match of objectives and activities to individual needs, and provide the agenda for whole setting evaluation.

Sound planning will enable practitioners to organise their own work so that they are able to achieve balance across and between the six areas of learning and experience. The balance in broad terms should be agreed through discussion about the entitlement for individual children, and practice should be checked to see that each child has proper access to all areas of learning and experience. The demands of ensuring

'Successful curriculum planning involves clear perceptions about the various objectives of the curriculum and how different activities can contribute to their achievement. But curriculum planning is not a once-and-for-all operation: it is a...

entitlement while protecting choice and freedom will be apparent to all involved!

Whole establishment planning is also how the setting formally addresses essential skills (e.g. language development, information skills, ICT, personal and social, and physical development) and tries to see that they are consistently addressed. It is in whole setting planning that the commitment to aims will be met, and a recognition of the contribution of each stage of the planned curriculum will be agreed.

Baseline assessments, monitored over time, will help to make sure that the map of learning experiences meets the needs of the children in the school, and the Stepping Stones now provide a useful national framework for this task. The information gathered will also help the setting to make adjustments according to the individual nature of the setting and the particular characteristics of groups and cohorts of children.

In Chapter 2 we included an example of a learning map for under fives which showed the key elements of the long term plan. They are written as broad outcome indicators of readiness to embark on the programmes of study for Key Stage 1, and include the *Early Learning Goals*.

...continuous cycle involving planning, observing, recording, assessing and returning to planning in the light of the intermediate stages.'

Starting with Quality, The Rumbold Committee, DES 1990.

The examples which follow may be photocopied or otherwise reproduced by purchasers of this book for use in their own institutions, subject to the same conditions set out in Chapter 2.

Example 1. Long Term Planning

Framework for mapping the learning experiences of children in a primary school

	Linguistic	Math-ematical	Knowledge & understanding of the world				Creative		Phys-ical	Personal & social development		
3+												
4+			Foundation Stage									
R												
	English	Maths	Science	D&T/ICT	History	Geog.	Music	Art	PE	RE	PSE	
Y1												
Y2												
Y3			Key Stages 1&2									
Y4												
Y5												
Y6												

Example 2. Medium term planning

In this example teachers use a double sided planner to record objectives for the thematic and core curriculum

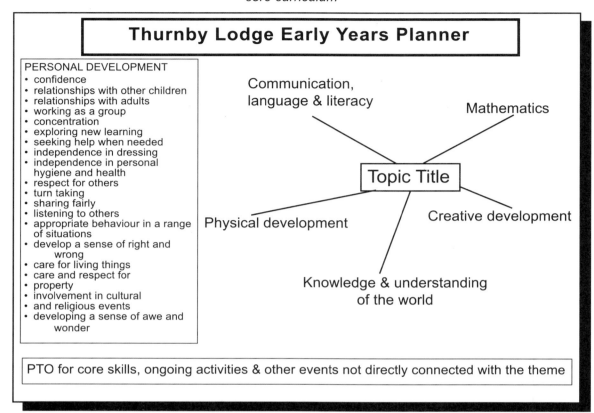

Thurnby Lodge Early Years Planner

PERSONAL DEVELOPMENT
- confidence
- relationships with other children
- relationships with adults
- working as a group
- concentration
- exploring new learning
- seeking help when needed
- independence in dressing
- independence in personal hygiene and health
- respect for others
- turn taking
- sharing fairly
- listening to others
- appropriate behaviour in a range of situations
- develop a sense of right and wrong
- care for living things
- care and respect for property
- involvement in cultural and religious events
- developing a sense of awe and wonder

Communication, language & literacy

Mathematics

Topic Title

Physical development

Creative development

Knowledge & understanding of the world

PTO for core skills, ongoing activities & other events not directly connected with the theme

Side 1

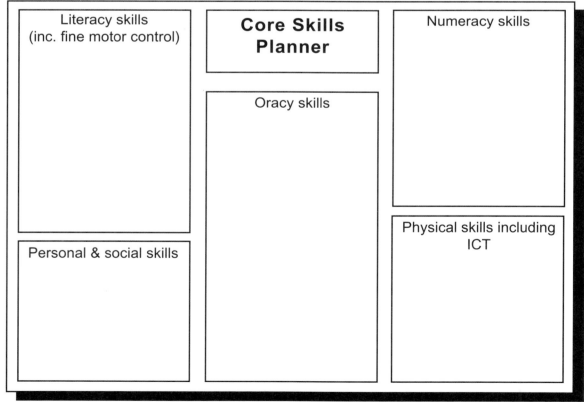

Literacy skills (inc. fine motor control)

Core Skills Planner

Numeracy skills

Oracy skills

Personal & social skills

Physical skills including ICT

Side 2

Example 3. Medium term planner for the Early Years

Area of learning	Medium Term Objectives	
Communication, language and literacy development	talking	
	books	
	mark making and writing	
Mathematical development		
Knowledge & understanding of the world	science	
	technology	
	ICT	
	sense of place	
	sense of time	
Creative development	art and craft	
	music	
	role play & drama	
Personal, social and emotional development		
Physical development - gross & fine motor skills (PE, DT, creative skills)	large motor skills	
	fine motor skills	
Other activities, visits, visitors, special occasions, celebrations		

This planner has been designed to recognise the different strands within the areas of learning and experience. It enables practitioners to ensure that each of the strands is given attention during each planning period.

This framework provides for the planning of learning outcomes and activities over a week or a fortnight. One type of use might be in a rotational programme, where activities are set up over a period of time and groups of children visit these in turn.(See also example 6)

Example 4. Medium term planner

Medium term planner	Timescale: summer term	Year: 2001	Theme: Minibeasts		
Area of learning & experience	Intended learning outcomes	Activities & experiences	Organisation & resources	Assessment	
Language & literacy					
Mathematical development					
Knowledge & understanding of the world					
Creative development					
Personal & social development					
Physical development					

Short term planning can take many forms, and schools have worked hard to devise those which suit them best. We include two examples, as suggestions – only you know what works best for you!

First Hand - making the Foundation Curriculum work

Example 5. Short term planner

This planner has a checklist on on the back which serves as an aide memoire for matching activities and their assessment to objectives.

Time/day/ session	What am I trying to teach? What do I want them to learn? (my objectives)	What is the activity? How will it be organised and differentiated? What resources will we use? What support is on offer? (the lesson plan)	Did they learn what I intended? How will I find out what they have learnt? (assessment)
	ELG		

side 2 - the checklist

Time/day/ session	What am I trying to teach? What do I want them to learn? (my objectives)	What is the activity? How will it be organised and differentiated? What resources will we use? What support is on offer? (the lesson plan)	Did they learn what I intended? How will I find out what they have learnt? (assessment)
	• practise ... • play with..... • explore..... • discover ... • understand ... • experience ... • estimate & check ... • listen to ... • watch ... • concentrate on ... • record ... • talk about ... • recognise & value ... • find out about ... • hypothesise ... • design/plan/make ... • test/evaluate ... • choose/select ... • organise ... • imagine ... • extend ... • work in a group/pair to ...	Groupings may be • whole group • mixed ability • ability • age • stage of development • individual • pairs • self selected • gender • peer • mixed ages Support by • additional adult • student • another practitioner • materials • resources • time • graded task	• observe ... • talk about ... • listen ... • question about ... • look at work ... • test by ... • mark ... • discuss with child ... • whole group discussion about ... • ask for demonstration of ... • ask for description of process ... • pupil evaluation of ... • adult set task ... • accumulation of other unrecorded evidence ...

Example 6. Skills planner (extract)

This planner was developed by the staff in a Nursery where rooms are allocated to different areas of the curriculum, and practitioners move round the rooms during the year. The planner attempts to ensure that children have opportunities to experience the widest possible range of materials and equipment in the widest possible range of settings. It should also ensure that activities are revisited on a regular basis to ensure progression in skills development.

This planner is one of five covering the four rooms in the setting, (the art and craft room also has a paint cycle). The other rooms are Science/Technology/ICT/Construction, the Garden and Language and Communication.

Weekly rotation - Art and craft room

	Malleable materials	Cut &stick	Cooking	Sand trays		Water tray
Week 1	clay and tools	catalogues, paste, spreaders	pastry (samosa/ chapatti)	wet sand no tools	dry sand, animals	colour, funnels, tubes
Week 2	dough, patty pans, cutters	paper strips for folding, glue & brushes	fruit or vegetables for cutting	sand and tools	beads	float and sink, either natural or plastic
Week 3	cooked pasta	ready cut shapes, glue, spreaders	drinks	gloop	dry sand, funnels, tubes	bubbles and blowers
Week 4	clay, no tools	magazines, card, glue sticks	buns or cake	sand and trucks	dry pasta, pans	ice shapes, colour
Week 5	dough and tools	fabric pieces, large card, joint project	exotic fruit or vegetables	wet sand, moulds	dry sand, dinosaurs	containers, spoons, bottles, jugs
Week 6	cooked pasta	coloured paper, zigzag scissors, glue sticks	biscuits, icing	slime	beads	colour, scented oil
Week 7	dough, no tools	cards, PVA glue	jelly, whip or custard	wet sand plastic cars	dry sand, people	tubes, pipes, funnels

Summary

- Planning is a whole setting activity, and is the means of achieving whole setting aims.
- Planning should ensure a curriculum which is rooted in first hand experiences and practical tasks.
- Plans are usually constructed in three layers – long, medium and short term. Each layer of planning informs and is informed by the others.
- Planning should balance flexibility and certainty. Plans need to be manageable, both in form and content.
- Planning should identify both core and thematic objectives.
- Planning should include time for observation, assessment and evaluation.
- Planning must recognise the unique nature of individuals and groups, and through systematic assessment should provide information for the next steps in learning by establishing clear targets for individuals and groups.

Chapter 6
Managing the curriculum

Teaching and learning

In earlier chapters we have advanced the view that children in the Foundation Stage have an entitlement to a planned, intentional curriculum based on the Areas of Experience, the Early Learning Goals and the Stepping Stones. We have given our view of what such a curriculum might contain and provided guidance and models for planning it. Now we come to the crucial role of the practitioner in supporting and extending chidlren's learning, and we start with the adults who are closest and most influential in this task.

In developing curriculum practice in the Early Years we must hold on to the principle that the learning and progress of the child should be at the centre of the decisions we make. This applies to particular individuals as well as to groups of children, so that the needs of everyone can be clearly recognised and so that all children genuinely have access to an appropriate, planned curriculum. In Chapter 1 we discussed the overall needs of children in the Early Years and suggested some principles which followed from them. These should now be the starting point for looking more closely at teaching and learning.

The role of the practitioner

We have seen (in Chapter 4) how the effective use of baseline and other assessment can help to ensure that an appropriate curriculum is available to all the children. There is a considerable body of research evidence to confirm that we should start from where the child is and provide learning opportunities through first hand experiences – hence the title we have taken for this book and its associated materials. Learning by doing is often a messy business! It also inevitably involves making mistakes. It is important to create an environment and atmosphere where children may make mistakes without fear of failure. The kind and degree of adult support which this demands will vary, depending on the previous experiences of the child. Where activities are routinely heavily prescribed the opportunity for what we term 'constructive error' is not available, and learning is therefore limited. The role of the adult is critical in promoting a positive attitude towards 'having a go'. Messages about success and failure are picked up very quickly by young children.

Play and talk are both powerful contributors to learning, not least because they can increase self-motivation and provide opportunities for the initiation of activities by the child. This is particularly important because one of our aims should be to develop children's independence as learners.

Although many children are by nature independent learners the constraints required by the organisation of the setting can often run counter to this. Promoting children's independence in learning requires careful planning and considerable commitment. This will be evident not only in the activities which are provided, but also in the way in which they are managed. It is worth thinking about not only how often children are given opportunities for choice in their activities but also, and even more important, whether they are truly able to make full use of that choice. There is a delicate balance to be achieved between the freedom to

First Hand - making the Foundation Curriculum work

choose and the encouragement – sometimes requirement – to do specific things at specific times.

Opportunities to choose make an important contribution to the development of decision making skills. However, choice can be offered in more ways than one. The adult can hand over some of the responsibility for carrying out a task while still making sure that the child has the support he or she needs. The child may have choices between one activity and another, over how to carry out the activity, about who to work with, which resources to use, and so on. The capabilities of young children should not be under-estimated in this regard. However, the opportunities to exercise choice should be presented in ways which help the child grow and develop, and not in ways which threaten security or create undue stress.

A good place to begin when reviewing your current practice is with these questions –

- What range of methods do we currently use?
- What types of activities do we provide?
- Do we achieve a balance of activities?
- How do we provide variety in the presentation of activities?
- Do we have a balance between adult-initiated tasks and those started by the child?
- What teaching styles do we use and in what situations?
- How do we cater for children's preferred styles of learning?
- How do we organise, allocate and use our time?
- Do we need to develop greater flexibility in our planning?
- Do we provide opportunities for spontaneity and choice?

The attitudes and expectations of both adults and children have a significant influence on curriculum practice. Adults working with young children should have shared, consistent and realistic expectations. This means communicating regularly with one another and asking questions about children's achievements. It is also important for adult expectations to be expressed clearly to children, and for the adult to understand the expectations of the child. This involves a considerable amount of conversation to allow adult and child to check each other over and reach common ground.

Sensitive adult intervention is the key to helping children as they move forward in their learning. Prior observation will enable decisions to be made about what level of intervention is needed. It may be as straight-forward as assisting with a difficult and potentially frustrating activity, such as threading a needle, thus enabling the child to maintain interest in the activity and to proceed as intended. It may encourage the development of a particular skill, such as observation, or extend the use of language. Careful, open questioning can stimulate thinking, problem-solving and decision-making, perhaps by referring back to previous learning and encouraging comparison with similar situations encountered in the past.

'What the child can do in co-operation today, he can do alone tomorrow.'

Mind and Society, Vygotsky 1978

'Good planning is essential for ensuring a broad, balanced and purposeful curriculum. As well as identifying what children should learn, curriculum plans need to take account of how it is intended that teaching and learning will take place.'

Looking at Children's Learning, SCAA 1997

'Working with young children is a demanding and complex task . Those engaged upon it need a range of attributes to assure a high quality of experience.'

Starting With Quality, HMSO 1990

Staffing

'An appropriate (staffing) ratio is one that allows adults to interact with the children and be involved with their activities, observing them as individuals and intervening at the right moment to extend their learning.'

Early to school – four year olds in infant classes, Cleave and Brown 1991

The degree to which the adult intervenes and participates in children's activities and the manner in which they do are equally crucial. As a participant the adult can act as a role model, for example in emergent writing by reinforcing the message that what matters is 'having a go', and that making mistakes is an understandable corollary of this. Adult participation can also extend the length of time over which children can concentrate and remain involved, as well as widening the scope of the activity itself.

Some of the most effective intervention is spontaneous, part of the wonderful serendipity which is one of the joys of teaching. Skilled teachers will always be on the look out for such opportunities. Other interventions should be planned, so that the adult is prepared for them and has time to assess what will be needed. We should not forget that there are, of course, occasions when non-intervention is the best course, giving time for the child(ren) to develop the activity and for the adult to stand back and observe.

Intervention will not always be by an adult; it may be by a peer in a collaborative activity, or by an older child in situations where there are opportunities for younger children to work alongside older pupils. What is critical is that the intervention helps the child to move on from what is already known into the new and unfamiliar – the area of further learning.

Staff appointments and staff development

If settings are to be sure that staff are properly equipped to meet the demands of the job, they will need to consider both the processes for the appointment of those who work with this age group and the opportunities and support provided for staff development.

It is important to consider what exactly the appointee will be expected to do, the sort of skills the responsibilities will require, and the qualification(s) and experience you are asking for. When staff are recruited there should be a clearly defined job description, together with a personnel specification and details which demonstrate the school's concern to attract someone with adequate initial training and an understanding of child development. Recruiting the right person can be an extremely difficult task. The government commitment to the expansion of provision for children of this age has had a marked effect on recruitment. Practitioners with the right skills and qualifications are in high demand.

Opportunities for professional development and refreshment are as important for new staff as they are for those who have been in post for some time. This is not just a matter of courses and staff meetings. There are many ways to provide for professional support and development.

Here are some of the elements you may wish to consider –

- regular staff discussions so that individuals understandtheir role and their responsibilities, and how these relate to others
- access to professional and self-support groups
- in-service training to update and develop skills
- formal and informal opportunities within setting to share good practice and expertise
- opprtunities to observe other practitioners at work
- opportunities within families of settings to share good practice and exchange views of developments
- team-based planning procedures where appropriate
- the construction pf a staff development plan, related to the needs of the whole setting as set out in its development plan and its improvement targets
- a system of appraisal or job evaluation
- a more informal process of feedback and regular professional discussion, which allows individuals at all levels to have access to co-workers and managers
- a system of appraisal or job evaluation
- a structured induction programme for newly qualified and newly appointed staff and for temporary cover

Parents students and other volunteers

The amount of parental help available to the school is inevitably subject to work patterns and other commitments. The nature of the setting, its ethos and sense of welcome will also affect the willingness of parents and other volunteers to become involved. However many or few are involved, parent helpers will appreciate the careful co-ordination of their efforts. This is usually best done by one member of staff.

The availability of student helpers will depend on proximity to and contacts with schools, colleges and training establishments. To get the best out of students and voluntary helpers and to ensure that their efforts are successful, it is important to have shared expectations of what they will do, and an agreed understanding of their role in the classroom and their relationship to other adults, including teachers. Volunteers should realise that, even though they *are* volunteers, they nevertheless have responsibilities to the children which will affect the way they conduct themselves, while working in the setting and outside. This is nowhere more true than in the matter of confidentiality. It is almost inevitable that volunteer helpers will overhear conversations about individuals and acquire knowledge of particular children. If you prepare for this by being clear about what you expect in such situations it will avoid difficulties later.

Volunteers, students and parents

'In the most successful work with four year olds, teachers and other adults closely monitored the children's activities and intervened purposefully.'

Aspects of Primary Education:
The Education of Children Under Five, HMI 1989.

Expectations should be clearly expressed to all volunteers in a way which is straightforward and accessible. They could take the form of simple, written guidelines, discussions or workshops. If everyone has the opportunity to talk about the expectations and to give their views there is a better chance of securing their co-operation. Avoid a list of 'do not's. Written guidelines should contain positive and useful information expressed in clear statements. They should promote the confidence of the volunteer and should not inhibit or overwhelm them – or confuse them with jargon. Above all, they should recognise the experience volunteers have and value what they can bring to the the experiences of the children.

Statements or sections to consider when drafting guidelines might include –

- commitment from all partners
- how to support children's learning
- responsibilities – e.g. time-keeping, attendance, personal presentation, dress, language and behaviour (including smoking)
- domestic arrangements – refreshments, cloakrooms, personal possessions, toilets, etc.
- health and safety issues, relating to themselves and to the children
- the implications of equal opportunities
- the confidentiality of information relating to individuals
- child protection issues (these need particularly sensitive handling)
- the possible range of activities in which they could be involved
- access to help, support and further advice
- opportunities for training
- relationships with other adults, and a named person who has particular responsibility for their work.

Organising the setting

The environment

The setting in which learning takes place includes not only the indoor but also the outdoor environment. Outdoor play is essential in order to meet the needs of young children for physical activity and the demands of the physical curriculum. *The Guidance for the Foundation Stage* stresses the need to 'plan and provide an environment that encourages children to do things, talk about what they are doing and think about how they can improve their actions and movements.' In considering indoor and outdoor environments you may find it helpful to look at the curriculum map in Chapter 2.

The indoor and outdoor environments combine together to provide the facilities which are needed for the Foundation curriculum. The successful use of both will be influenced by a number of factors which include –

- planning – to ensure balance within the range of activities
- responsibilities – so that each adult understands her or his role
- skills and specialisms – to make the most of what each adult has to offer
- allocation of staff to activities – to ensure adequate supervision
- use of rotas – so that everyone takes their turn
- timetables – to make best use of time and facilities
- the needs of the rest of the setting – to avoid competing demands from other age groups.

Although each situation will be different in its size, resources, layout and range of provision, there is a common need to ensure adequate safety and security. In the outdoor environment this includes gates, fences, surfaces and equipment. Each of these should be subject to regular checks, with a clear procedure available for all adults to report hazards and potential problems as they arise. *First Hand – auditing the curriculum for under fives*, which is a companion to this book, is a source of useful help in this task.

Ideally there should be a range of surfaces available for children in the outdoor environment, giving them access to grass and to hard and soft areas for different types of play. This may have implications for the level of supervision which is required, and you may have to decide whether it is practical to allow access to all surfaces all the time. You will also need to think about how you can make sure that all children have equal opportunities to use the outdoor environment. Factors to consider here include –

- the amount of freedom of movement between indoors and outdoors
- the amount of free choice children have in this movement
- any need for timetabling access to outdoor facilities
- the balance between indoor and outdoor activities and the amount of time spent on each.

The outdoor environment is not simply 'the place where the children play'. It offers resources and experiences which are an essential part of children's learning. It is crucial to have a clear understanding among staff of the value and purpose of the out door environment, and how these relate to overall curriculum aims. It may also be necessary to discuss, and perhaps take action to modify, children's perceptions of the outdoor environment if they are to benefit fully from the experiences which it can provide. Outdoor play is not simply recreational, it is part of the planned learning environment.

'The setting in which learning takes place is crucial to the quality of the provision.'

Education 3-5:
A Teachers Handbook,
M. Dowling 1988

Turning to the indoor environment raises other factors which can influence Early Years curriculum provision and practice. Again, situations differ, but there are significant common elements. Obviously the actual accommodation is important, not only in terms of the amount of space available but also in the potential to create areas for different types of activities. Ideally there should be enough room for several things to be going on without interfering with or distracting each other. The area(s) need to be able to cater for a variety of activities of different types – moving/static, able spaces can be used, and there should be a range of surfaces suitable for different purposes. While there is probably little you can do in the short term about the location of the indoor environment and the spaces it provides, it will be worth looking at the Early Years accommodation in relation to other facilities (e.g. toilets, outdoor areas) and amenities such as the hall or library. It may be possible to find ways of improving access to these, perhaps through negotiation with colleagues.

You will also need to think about the way the accommodation is furnished – age and condition, suitability, size and so on. Changing, adding and removing items can all help you to shape the environment to suit varying purposes. Storage facilities are often a problem, but if you are aiming to develop children's independence it is important that resources are stored in ways which will enable them to have safe access. Equally, there may be a need for some items to be in inaccessible places!

Inevitably there are some experiences which cannot be provided on the premises, either indoors or out, and consideration should to be given to the part trips and visits are to play in the Early Years curriculum. These may be close (e.g. visits to the library, shops, places of worship, local play area) or further afield (art gallery, farm park, museum, theatre).

Equipment and materials

Resources

The curriculum map in Chapter 2 suggests some of the resources needed to provide the range of activities and experiences to which we believe children should have access in their Early Years. There is no doubt that materials and equipment for this age group can be very expensive. Moreover, however well they are cared for they will need regular updating and replacement. If you have not already done so, you may find it useful to review your existing resources. *First Hand – auditing the curriculum for under fives* contains a series of questions to help you assess the range, adequacy, sufficiency, accessibility and maintenance of your resources. From these you can identify priorities for action.

It is also useful to reach agreement within your setting and among the Early Years team on some general issues which affect the development of resource provision. A clear understanding will help you to achieve consistency about what you make available for children to use. Start by clarifying who is empowered to decide what new resources will be purchased and when. In most situations several people will play a part – for example, all adults working within the setting, the co-ordinator for Early Years, a subject specialist who selects resources for the whole school, the setting manager or owner, parent groups, and sometimes the children. The person with overall responsibility for the setting will probably have the final say. Whoever makes the decisions, what is important is that the choice supports curriculum provision and enables the planned activities to be carried out effectively. Depending on individual circumstances it may be possible to access a variety of sources of funding – government or local grants, charities, money raised by parents or sponsorship from local business.

It is also important to agree the level of quality of the resources which you aim to provide in both the indoor and outdoor environments. This will help when making decisions about what to buy, and in time will set a consistent standard of provision throughout the setting. There needs to be consensus about when and where you will provide real materials for children to use and when (if appropriate) you will employ commercially produced replicas. In some situations you may feel the need to supplement your existing resources with home-made, second hand or found materials. An agreement about quality will set the standard for what is and is not acceptable and appropriate. Whatever source is used, the intention should always be to provide children with the best possible equipment available in the circumstances.

Looking at resources in this way can be a useful starting point for your discussion of Early Years curriculum practice because it offers a pragmatic approach based on what you already have. This can lead into the process of looking in depth at how, as adults, you present learning opportunities to children.

Health and safety

There are a number of health and safety issues which need to be considered specifically in relation to this age group. These are essential in order to allow the child to experience the curriculum and the activities which have been planned in a safe environment. In matters of health and safety it is impossible to be too careful. We recommend a separate audit of the health and safety issues which arise from your curriculum planning and your review of provision, and that these are recorded, preferably as a separate document as well as being incorporated within the Health and Safety policy for the whole setting. We suggest you consider all of the following headings and how they apply to the issues identified within your own working environment. You may wish to add further headings of your own. Again, *First Hand – auditing the curriculum for under fives* will give you some useful pointers.

'It is important that the resources in the classroom provide opportunities for the development of the whole child and encourage children to become independent and confident'.

Early to school – Four year olds in infant classes, Cleave and Brown 1991

Health and safety issues

Health and safety - Staffing

The adult:child ratio may vary according to the type of activity and where it is taking place – e.g. outdoor play, cookery or indoor PE need more adult supervision than telling a story to the whole group. It is important to be aware of this, and to plan the adult involvement by recording who is counted in the adult:child ratio. The times when people are available, particularly volunteer helpers, will probably influence when you plan for various activities to take place. It should also be clear to everyone who is the person with overall responsibility. You may want to make a separate reference to the arrangements for supervision at the beginning and end of the day and, where needed, at lunchtimes.

Health and safety - Facilities

This section refers particularly to the different locations used by the children within the building, and the purposes for which they are available. You will also need to consider the outdoor environment, particularly gates, safety surfaces, fences and other potential hazards. You should identify any areas of potential danger and the actions required of adults to ensure that the children are safe, both inside and outside the building. Children need to be taught the importance of safety from the earliest possible opportunity, and we suggest you pay particular attention to the movement and supervision of children between different locations, so that they become familiar with safe and consistent practice. Do not forget to include toilet facilities in your assessment, with a record of adequacy and expected standards of cleanliness and hygiene.

Health and safety - Resources

A review of your resources will concentrate on materials and equipment which have the potential to cause damage or injury, and on how you intend to teach the children to use them safely. It will be important to ensure that everyone is clear about the safety standards of equipment and how they can be maintained. This should include reference to the matters such as hygiene, the maintenance of equipment and the different roles of children and adults. Examples of activities you might specify in order to develop good habits of health and safety could be training children to put sand which has been swept up in the waste bin rather than back in the sand tray, or to report spills promptly to an adult so that they can be dealt with properly. The arrangements for the setting out and tidying of equipment will also need consideration, particularly where there is a risk involved. There should be a routine for checking all equipment for deterioration.

Health and safety - Clothing

Depending on your particular circumstances, you may wish to

include brief statements about appropriate clothing for indoor activities, outdoor activities and PE. Reference to jewellery will need to be dealt with sensitively where cultural differences exist.

Health and safety - Procedures

It is always better to anticipate difficulties and plan for them before they arise. Again, although each situation is different, we recommend that the following points are considered and discussed, and that in each case all the adults involved know the procedures agreed.

- The arrangements for reporting and dealing with dangerous items of equipment and hazards in the building.
- Accident and incident procedures.
- First Aid – the location of kits and the names of qualified first aiders.
- Fire procedures – including clear arrangements for the swift evacuation of the building in the case of a fire or other emergency.
- What should happen when a child is sick and needs to be withdrawn from the rest of the group.
- What should happen when a child has an accident which requires the changing of clothes.
- The arrangements for monitoring visitors and regulating who has access to the building, and when.
- Emergency contacts with parents – details of where and how parents can be reached in an emergency, and the whereabouts of these lists so that they can be found in a hurry.
- The arrangements for securing parental consent for visits, walks and other trips out of the usual environment.
- The action to be taken on those occasions when an individual with key responsibilities for the safety of children is absent.

Governors/managers

In considering the management of the setting, it is important to consider the place of governors or the management committee. In meeting its responsibilities for the setting, such a body needs to have a clear view of its role and what that means in a practical sense. This involves looking at its statutory obligations as well as the potential for useful involvement in the everyday life of the setting and support for the work going on there.

While some governors/managers may prefer to keep a certain distance between themselves and the setting, the best management bodies work hard to develop an interest in and an understanding of education and the work of the practitioners. This applies no less to the Early Years than to the later stages of education.

The role of governors and managers of settings

The role of the governor is 'to provide a strategic view of where the school is heading; to act as a critical friend to the school; and to hold the school to account for the educational standards it achieves and the quality of education it provides.'

Guidance for the inspection of Nursery and Primary schools, OFSTED

Such involvement is often demonstrated by the nomination of a specialist governor or manager with the responsibility of being well informed on issues relating to the Foundation Stage. This person can also provide a focal point for support for the senior managers and for the staff, demonstrating the commitment of the management body to Early Years education.

At a practical level governors and managers can strengthen their relationship with Early Years staff by attending events, making visits, offering classroom support and assisting with celebrations, outings and visits. Participation of this sort will increase their knowledge and experience of the setting they manage. This knowledge is vital to enable positive action in securing the best possible provision for this age group and making informed representation to the LEA and other bodies.

This chapter has underlined the huge range of responsibilities held by practitioners and those who manage them. There could be a pressure to concentrate on the mechanics of health and safety or the condition of the equipment, but we must not forget that the most important difference that a setting can make to the experiences of chidlren is the quality of relationships and the sensitivity of the practitioners' intervention.

Summary

- Successful management of the Early Years curriculum requires the knowledgeable commitment of all the adults involved in every aspect of school life.
- Decisions about teaching and learning in the Early Years should be based on a thorough assessment of the needs of young children.
- The Early Years curriculum is an integral part of the whole curriculum, and should be understood by those who work with other age groups.
- The governing/managing body should take action to inform itself about Early Years issues, in order to carry out its statutory responsibilities and provide the right support for the school.
- There should be enough suitably trained staff with the qualifications and experience to structure and support the learning of young children effectively.
- The Early Years setting should include both the indoor and outdoor environments, with resources appropriate to a wide range of activities.
- Health and Safety issues must be considered specifically in relation to Early Years provision, responding to the needs of the age group.

Chapter 7

Involving others

The previous chapter explored the management of the curriculum for the under fives and included guidance on working with volunteers, students and parents. In this chapter we look in more detail at ways in which schools can involve parents, the community, specialists and other services to support the Early Years curriculum, and the reasons why this is important.

Parents

'Parents are children's first and most enduring educators. When parents and practitioners work together in early years settings, the results have a positive impact on the child's development and learning. Therefore, each setting should seek to develop an effective partnership with parents.

Curriculum Guidance for the Foundation Stage, QCA 2000

The phrase 'parents are a child's first teachers' is no less valid for being often quoted. There is ample evidence and experience to show that children's education is almost always improved when their parents not only show an interest in what they are learning but also give active support, and that this is most effective when it is done in partnership with the providers of the learning. Parents have varying amounts of time and different levels of interest and skills which they are able to bring to this role. The task for the setting and its practitioners is to provide a situation which encourages parental involvement and allows parents to contribute in the ways which suit their personal wishes and circumstances best.

In looking at the common features of good practice, QCA (2000) has made a number of recommendations about involving parents as partners. They are based on the understanding that partnership needs to be a two-way process which enables adults to share their knowledge and skills in an atmosphere of welcome and mutual respect.

We can consider the setting's relationship with parents in three overlapping areas: the support they provide at home, the information and guidance they need from teachers or carers and their involvement in the classroom.

The first contact with parents needs to be early. Before the child is admitted there should be arrangements in place for initial contacts, pre-visits, induction, home visits and meetings. You may choose to emphasise one or two of these rather than all, depending on your own circumstances and the needs of the families in your area. Whatever method you choose, your overall aim will be to ensure as smooth a start as possible for both child and family, building on your experience of what works for you. This early contact will probably include providing parents with written information about the setting, its aims, principles and characteristics, and something about the expectations and obligations on both sides. All settings receiving government funding for three and fur year olds must by law produce a prospectus or handbook, and many now supplement this with specific information and guidance for the families of pre-school children. Experience suggests that such information is particularly useful and well received when parents are invited to give advice on its content, or sometimes even write it themselves for other prospective parents.

The purpose of the arrangements is to encourage an early dialogue with parents in order to support the child through the important changes in his or her life that starting school or nursery will bring. This dialogue should form the starting point for the collection of the baseline information discussed in Chapter 4, and lead to the agreement of initial targets when the child starts school. Ideally, this will be the first of many discussions that staff and parents have about the child's learning, and practitioners should not forget to plan arrangements for reviewing what progress has been made in the light of those first targets, and the ones which follow.

The early information for parents will need to be supplemented later. However, the way in which this is done need not always be formal. Parents often place the highest value on the regular, informal contact with practitioners which occurs when bringing or collecting the child at the beginning or end of the session. This is a valuable point of contact which can be usefully supplemented by a parents' noticeboard in some convenient location, inside the setting or out. If you are lucky enough to have a parents' room it can be used as a meeting place and as a library where other information for parents can be located. Parents' understanding of how the setting works is built up over time, not least by word of mouth! Notice of present and future activities, posters, photo books, charts showing the plan of what classes and groups will be doing, tips, reminders and general information will all help. However, nothing discourages readers more than a dull and unchanging display of mostly outdated material. If it is to communicate well and be of real value, the noticeboard needs to be carefully maintained and changed often. That is a time-consuming job for somebody, but one that is well worth doing. Of course, even the best managed notice board will not reach all parents, and there is still a need for routine newsletters, specific written information and guidelines.

There are many opportunities for involving parents in the life of the school or nursery. They will depend on the individual characteristics of the setting and its catchment. It is helpful to start as soon as possible after the child begins to attend, and some institutions make a point of running a parents' workshop early in the year to encourage parents to become active partners. Workshops are more effective when they have a specific focus – e.g. reading, managing behaviour, or encouraging early learning activities at home – but they should also offer plenty of opportunities for parents to ask questions and raise matters which concern them, and a cup of coffee often serves to break the ice!

Parental involvement in the classroom and in outside activities such as visits, walks and swimming can be of great benefit to all concerned. It is not simply a matter of the parent being an additional adult supervisor or helper. The value of parents joining in with what the children are doing is that it gives them an insight into the work of the setting. Even more important is that it provides parent and child with a shared experience which can be a topic of conversation after the event is over, when the learning can be reviewed and reinforced.

Naturally, much depends on how much time a parent has available. With the best will in the world, some may not be able to contribute to

'... parental involvement does not merely contribute to quality but is essential if early education is to be successful'.

Education Provision for the Under Fives, HMSO 1989.

the daytime work of the setting at all. Others may prefer not to be involved in the classroom but would rather help with fund-raising, in the library or bookshop, or even with clerical tasks in the office. Volunteer help of this sort requires careful management, and we refer you to the related discussion in Chapter 6. Welcome as such help is, it is important not to regard the various offers merely as a free resource. Its main value is in the opportunity it gives to the setting to communicate its work and its aims to the community.

Parents whose commitments – or inclinations – prevent a high degree of involvement can still support the school. Many parents are prepared to come to school functions such as sports days, concerts or drama performances, especially if their own child is taking part. You might like to invite parents to an assembly or work sharing sometimes, or to be present at story time. These contacts should be seen by you as opportunities to plan and encourage further contact. A single visit like this has often led to a parent becoming connected with the work of the setting on a regular basis.

Some parents may be willing to become a member of the governing body or the management committee. Donating their skills and taking on specific responsibilities in this way offers them a more formal part in the development of the school and a shared responsibility for the standards it achieves. It will also give them a voice in the management of provision and the establishment of policies. These parents can, for example, respond to consultations or questionnaires, participate in discussions or act as a critical reader for the papers and documents intended for other parents or the public.

Links with parents need to be managed, and the importance of this should not be under estimated. It is a good idea for a designated member of staff to have responsibility for the co-ordination of work with parents. Part of this role is the management of the shared approach to community involvement set out in the setting's policy statement (see Chapter 3).

Community links

The development of links with the community is beneficial in many ways, not least in extending children's experiences beyond the immediate and in helping to promote knowledge and understanding of the world. Parents are a major element in the community and will be the schools most direct and frequently employed channel. However, many Early Years providers will want to exploit the opportunities offered by the wider community. These, even more than links with parents, will depend on the context in which the setting operates.

Visits to local shops and businesses increase children's awareness of the environment and what adults do when they go to work. It may be possible to establish contacts with individuals who are prepared to share an experience, a particular skill, craft or occupation. It goes without saying that these visits require careful planning and organisation. Children need to be well prepared, and the visits themselves should be

First Hand - making the Foundation Curriculum work

brief and focused. Ideally they should take place in the morning, to allow time later in the day to talk with the children about the visit so that they can internalise the event and gain the most benefit from the learning opportunities it presents, playing out the experiences with others and talking with adults about what thye have seen.

Visits to other schools, playgroups and nurseries give children the chance to have contact with others in different settings. This broadens their experience and can develop into regular exchanges to provide a stimulus and focus for other learning activities. In addition, the chances provided for liaison between adults should not be overlooked. Some of the benefits of this adult exchange of ideas and experience are considered in Chapter 6.

There are a number of other ways in which settings can interact with the community. Faith groups and places of worship may be able to increase children's awareness of other cultures and beliefs. Charities may form a link with the school, and community projects may enable children to make a visible contribution to the local area by, for example, planting bulbs, collecting litter or making posters. If there is a local group or home for the elderly it may be possible to make links with older members of the community. In these days of greater social mobility many children live at some distance from grandparents. Meeting and talking with old people can be of great benefit in helping children understand differences between then and now, and in appreciating the variety of life.

'Children are more likely to be interested in adult occupations when they can see adults at work, look at the machines and equipment they use, talk to them about what they do and listen to what they have to tell.'

Curriculum Matters 7, HMSO 1986

Early Years providers should be able to draw upon a range of different services to support their work with young children. Referral and formal support may be needed for an individual child or family, and it is really useful to keep an up to date database of available help, as well as maintaining a regular telephone contact if possible. Written information for all staff should include a list of available support, together with the procedures for making contact or referral. In order to deal effectively with outside groups and agencies, you might consider allocating this responsibility to a member (or members) of staff. A named person within the setting and a clear procedure for contact will help to ensure smooth links with other agencies. Building sound external relationships can prove invaluable when advice is needed.

Specialists and other services

'To promote mutual support, schools with children under five should seek links with other agencies working with young children and their families so that knowledge and expertise can be shared.'

Early to School – four year olds in infant classes, Cleave and Brown 1991

Situations vary, but within each community there should be a range of complementary skills and knowledge upon which the setting is able to draw. These include –

- health workers, (including the school and community health services)
- the educational psychological service
- special needs teams, including speech therapists and those who work with hearing impaired or partially sighted children
- the library and information service
- social services
- emergency services (police, ambulance, fire)

- local voluntary groups and community workers
- religious representatives
- home-school liaison officers and education welfare officers
- road safety officers
- INSET providers and consultants
- teacher trainers, colleges and higher education institutions
- LEA advisers, inspectors and advisory teachers with Early Years experience, officers and support services

Links can be made in a number of ways. Visits to local facilities such as the library or fire station can extend children's first hand experience, which can be further expanded by later discussion and re-visit. Visitors to the setting can bring with them experiences, stories and artefacts which will support and stimulate learning. The opportunity for talk on these occasions is often considerable. Contacts need not be formal. Regular and informal visits by, for example, the local police officer will help in building a relationship with young children over a long period.

No setting, however perfect can expect to work in isolation from the information, help and advice it can receive from others. Parents, professional bodies and the local community all have an important part to play in the education of our children by helping us ensure that the curriculum is broad, relevant, based on experiences of life in the world beyond school, and has specialist support readily available when it is needed. Schools and other settings for under fives have a responsibility to maintain a structure that enables this to happen.

Summary

- The partnership between practitioners and parents should be a two way process which enables the sharing of knowledge, expertise and information.
- Parental involvement can take many forms, and benefits from sensitive matching of skills, tasks and individuals
- Community involvement broadens the experience of children and enables the setting to function more effectively in the wider context.
- Links with other settings are an essential part of the support network for both adults and children.
- Access to a wide range of specialist support will be easier if an up to date directory of available sources is maintained.
- The management of community and specialist work within the setting will benefit from the identification of clear roles and responsibilities, together with a structure for the management and development of relationships.

'There can be no better breeding ground for children to develop... than when brought face to face with the real world, where there is real action, and alongside a challenging teacher who is determined to build up his children's' personal autonomy and social responsibility...'

Schools Council Occasional Bulletin (Art 7-11) HMSO 1978

First Hand - making the Foundation Curriculum work

Chapter 8

Monitoring and evaluation

All conscientious professionals examine their own practice, and so do you. The fact that you are reading this book demonstrates your willingness to examine your practice and evaluate what you do against the models we describe. However, there is a difference between informal and personal evaluation and the systematic, rigorous and public model demanded by the new pressures of national and local expectations, OFSTED, appraisal, target setting and performance related pay.

Monitoring and evaluating involves us in asking questions about our work and acting on the answers. Sometimes the answers will give us confidence that our work is effective, that we are fulfilling our objectives and that children are benefiting from their experiences with us. Sometimes the answers will challenge us and give us reason to reconsider our principles and practice. We may find that what we say in our documentation is not what we do in reality. We may find that groups or individuals are not getting the curriculum we intend or the range of activities we have planned. Usually the answers will pose more questions and set more targets for improvement. In any event, we must base our development work on knowledge of what is actually experienced by children and how they respond to it.

The present culture of our society is one of accountability. Accountability rests on evidence – what Brent Davies calls 'the need to prove the improvement.' If we leave judgements about the effectiveness of what we do entirely to bodies outside the school (inspectors, the media, etc.) we lack control over our work and risk being misunderstood and becoming demoralised. The answer is to balance the external view with a rigorous and thorough internal examination of the setting– a real knowledge of whether what we say really *is* what we do.

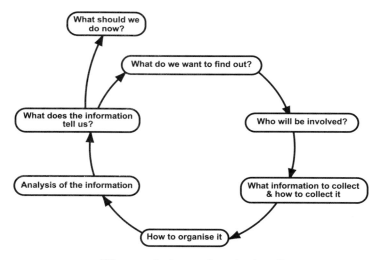

Monitoring and evaluation - the process

What should we do now?

What do we want to find out?

What does the information tell us?

Who will be involved?

Analysis of the information

What information to collect & how to collect it

How to organise it

Who can help us at each stage?

There are a number of models for self review. In this chapter we examine the different levels of monitoring and evaluation, starting with our own close examination of teaching and learning, moving through other internal methods, the involvement of others as critical friends and the external and objective model of OFSTED inspections.

Sharply focused monitoring needs time, clear focus and criteria and a commitment from everyone. Whichever methods are used, schools and other providers should avoid the tendency to think that systematic monitoring and evaluation should be happening everywhere all the time. If we do that there is no time for teaching and learning!

It can be argued that observation of teaching and learning by practitioners themselves is the most valuable and honest evaluation of practice. It has the potential to yield the most useful information because it is close to the child and the teacher in action. However, it has disadvantages too.

Advantages

- It is first hand, giving an insight into what really goes on in the setting.
- The observers are familiar to staff and children.
- The stress of being observed is more manageable.
- The observers know and understand the philosophy and context of the setting.
- The timing, criteria and focus can be negotiated.

Disadvantages

- The criteria are sometimes woolly.
- It is possible to use this method to confirm strengths without identifying weaknesses, leading to complacency.
- It is sometimes difficult to be constructively critical of someone you know well.
- It is expensive of time and cover for the observer.
- Practitioners may lack experience in observation.
- Finding time to do it can cause problems.

Tips for success

- Try observing yourself to start with. Some people set up a video recorder in a corner of the room, so they can watch themselves later in private. Others use an observation sheet as they work.
- Try pairing for observations – 'I'll show you mine if you show me yours.'
- Start within teams or groups, or choose someone you know and trust for the first observations
- Use a framework, such as the 6 observation questions on the right.
- Don't observe for too long, or too often.

'Good schools are engaged in a continuous review of their strengths and weaknesses'

Making the most of Inspection, OFSTED 1995

School based strategies – the classroom observed by the teacher

Questions for observation –
1. What did the children actually do?
2. What were they learning?
3. How worthwhile was it?
4. What did I do?
5. What did I learn?
6. What do I intend to do now?

A Teachers' Guide to Curriculum Review, Leicestershire LEA 1976

- Record what you see (monitoring), then give yourself some time before feedback to write what you think the observation is telling you (evaluation).
- Agree some simple criteria (there are examples in Appendix 4).
- Use an agreed recording sheet.
- Make time for feedback and try to be fair but honest, using the criteria you have agreed. Try to feed back positive comments as well as problems. Be honest about the difficulties of being observed and being an observer.
- If you can afford it, try working in a trio with someone who has some experience in observation (e.g. a colleague, adviser or consultant).

Looking at documentation

Another way into monitoring and evaluation is by **looking at documentation**. Many settings now have a cycle, usually covering several years, of monitoring and evaluating the effectiveness of their curriculum aims and principles, their schemes of work, planning, assessment and record keeping.

Written documents are a public statement of intent, and regular reviews of whether what you say is what you do are very important. Such reviews can –

- answer questions
  (e.g. Do parents understand what we write in reports? Is every child getting experience of poetry? Do children in parallel groups get an equivalent curriculum?)
- challenge judgements
  (e.g. The OFSTED report states that practitioners are not using classroom assessment to inform planning. Is this so? How can we find out? If it is true, what should we do?)
- check assumptions
  (e.g. Is our health and safety policy in place? Do we agree on what constitutes an active, practical curriculum?)
- identify strengths and needs in teaching
  (e.g. Are we now more confident in teaching IT since the training session for all Early Years staff?)

Reviews of documentation are one step away from the children, while remaining within the setting.

Advantages

- It is a simple way of reminding ourselves of what we are trying to do.
- It is cheaper in time and cover than direct observation. Some settings use a workshop approach during a training session to look at one document in detail or several in groups.
- It enables staff to know where practice may not be matching intentions *before* an external review takes place.
- It helps with the induction of new staff.

First Hand - making the Foundation Curriculum work

Disadvantages

- It is based on what people think rather than on first hand observation in the classroom.
- It can take a long time to get through all the documents!
- There is often a resistance to changing documentation once it has been constructed.
- This method is a long way from the experiences of children – good documentation does not necessarily mean good practice, and vice versa.

Tips for success

- Take it slowly. Don't take things for granted. Check up on them.
- Don't assume that review will necessarily (or even usually) mean re-writing.
- Try to be objective.
- If you don't know the answer, use observation to find out.
- Focus on positives, but be realistic about what needs doing.
- Date or record the review as part of the documentation.
- Involve as many people as possible.

Balance between adult directed and child initiated activities, outdoor play, access, independent learning are all possible areas to consider when **looking at the mechanics of the curriculum**.

Questions might be –

- Do we give equal emphasis and value to all activities and areas of the curriculum?
- Do children spend a balanced amount of time on different activities?
- Do we use a wide range of groupings and organisation?
- Do we use all resources, equipment and spaces fully?
- Are boys and girls getting equal treatment?
- Do SEN children get the entitlement we would wish?
- Does our curriculum meet the needs of all children?

Methods might include –

- tracking children or adults
- checking planning against the curriculum map or documents
- questionnaires
- equipment checks
- spot checks on space and time
- self checks of groups and organisation
- discussions with children

Advantages

- This is a relatively cheap method, particularly if you use self checks and discussions.
- The method brings you close to the action and the learning.
- The method confirms that we mean what we say.
- It gives us a flavour of what an individual child experiences.

Looking at the mechanics of the curriculum

Disadvantages

- Judgements can be subjective so they need a firm evidence base, not just opinion or hearsay.
- This method, too, can be a long way from the experiences of children. Again, good documentation does not necessarily mean good practice.

Tips for success

- Develop a vigilant attitude.
- Use checklists and grids to ensure coverage when planning.
- Talk to other people about it.
- Don't become a clock watcher!

Looking at the work of children

An effective and important way to monitor and evaluate what is happening in the Early Years is to look at **the work the children do and have done**. This can include the use of video, tape and photos, and discussing what they are telling us that children know and can do. Monitoring and evaluating in this way is close to the children and can often yield real insights into what they are learning.

Advantages

- It is relatively cheap, especially if you use meeting time or training sessions.
- The information is easily available.
- The focus is on learning and achievement, not on planning.

Disadvantages

- Collecting information on practical activities is difficult. There is a danger that we will only recognise what the child can write or draw, rather than what they can *do*.
- Judgements can be subjective; we see what we want to see.
- Comparisons are within the setting and may lack an objective perspective.

Tips for success

- Get examples from all areas of the curriculum and all activities.
- Use clear criteria for evaluating attainment.
- Try using samples, photos, video from other settings.

'There is a variety of ways in which these goals can be achieved, and settings need to review their approaches to teaching and learning to ensure that their curriculum is of a high quality and likely to promote the Desirable Outcomes in all six areas of learning.'

Looking at Children's Learning, SCAA 1997

The analysis of statistics

The analysis of statistics is increasingly favoured by some as the starting point for the evaluation of effectiveness. If done thoroughly it can enable a calculation of 'added value'. Judgements of the effectiveness of schools and other settings must be based on knowledge of the unique features of each establishment. Some relevant ones might be –

- the number of children who have English as an additional language
- the number of children with special educational needs

- families with no adult in work
- levels of spoken language
- attainment of previous years against the Early Learning Goals
- school attainment at Year 2 in national assessments

Advantages

- Statistics can be used to justify or explain levels of attainment.
- Such analysis is relatively easy to undertake and inexpensive of time, provided that you don't let it get out of hand.
- Statistical evidence forms part of the evidence base for an inspection, so knowing the figures will help you to prepare.
- Statistics sometimes surprise us, so we should look at them regularly to see what they tell us.

Disadvantages

- Statistical analysis can be misleading, and can be used as an excuse for under performance.
- Tests for very young children are notoriously insecure.
- Statistics can be used to prove almost anything. ('There are lies, damned lies, and statistics!')
- Statistical analysis can become a very time consuming hobby!

Tips for success

- Make sure you collect all the available, relevant information.
- Remain aware of the limitations of statistics.
- Be honest and objective when looking at results. It's easy to ignore messages you don't believe or don't want to see.
- Use other methods to amplify the evidence and confirm (or modify) your judgements.

Visits to other classes, schools and settings

Time spent in someone else's room or setting gives a real insight into how children learn and teachers teach. It is helpful if you can arrange to see other groups within your setting. Harder to organise but potentially even more valuable is to visit classes in other schools and other Early Years settings.

Visits by teachers to exhibitions, libraries, displays of equipment and materials, resource centres and educational suppliers are also useful, particularly in updating ideas and equipment.

Advantages

- You are seeing a real practitioner at work.
- You will get practical ideas of how to improve and extend your own practice.
- You will certainly find some things which make you feel pleased or confident about your own practice!

Disadvantages

- It is expensive, because it has to happen in session time and

'There can be no improvement without the teacher. Teacher development and student development are reciprocally related. We therefore suggest that a good proportion of ...

Professional development discussions and appraisal

someone has to cover your job. You need to be selective and have a clear purpose for your visit.

- You may sometimes feel disheartened about the work you still have to do.

Tips for success

- Agree your criteria for the visit before you go – otherwise you will not make the best use of it.
- Don't try to take in too much. Decide what you want to look at, and concentrate on that.
- Choose settings which resemble your own.

Professional development discussions and appraisal are another way of monitoring. The focus is on teaching, identifying strengths and weaknesses. The best appraisals leave practitioners feeling valued, respected and supported while giving them clear and agreed targets for their further development as professionals.

Many settings have limited resources for appraisal, but most can now provide an opportunity for all staff to discuss their jobs with an appraiser. Usually this is a more experienced member of the staff. At their best such discussions recognise success and identify training needs.

Advantages

- You have a specific time for discussion, with or without classroom observation.
- You have a chance to reflect on the things that have gone well and those which have not been so successful.
- It provides an opportunity to identify and plan training and support.
- It gives people a reason for looking at each other's practice.

Disadvantages

- It is expensive of time.
- If not sensitively handled it can feel threatening.
- It can be frustrating and unhelpful if not given the priority it deserves.

Tips for success

- Be clear about the purpose of the activity.
- Use a shared agenda for the appraisal, which has been agreed beforehand, so that everyone involved knows what to expect and can prepare for it accordingly.
- Be punctilious about confidentiality.
- Use it as a positive opportunity to discuss your job and ask for help in areas where you think you need it.

'External perspectives - Inspection

School self evaluation should complement the thorough but occasional health check provided by inspection.' - *OFSTED 1998*

Inspection is one of the most powerful influences in schools and other child care settings today. The announcement of an inspection can send everyone into a panic and the process can leave everyone exhausted, even in the most successful settings. At its best, OFSTED inspection offers valuable consultancy, an evaluation of the school by trusted and respected professionals. It is a high profile activity with a public report which can provide confirmation of good practice in teaching, learning and management, or surprise you with evidence of things you never knew were happening.

The secret of managing a successful inspection is to know your own setting well. If you are undertaking regular monitoring and evaluation, you will know your strengths and weaknesses and the inspection report will contain no surprises. If your development plan addresses Early Years priorities, and monitoring and evaluation is a regular feature of practice, the staff should be able to tell the inspection team what the report will say.

The attitude of the staff is crucial to making the most of the inspection process and to a positive reception of its judgements. The headteacher or manager of the provision, the governors and staff have the responsibility for addressing the issues raised in the report. In the best situations these issues are already part of the development plan because they have resulted from regular and thorough self review.

Nursery inspections are part of the national inspection system, and the criteria for the inspection of nursery schools and classes are contained in OFSTED's *Framework for the Inspection of Schools* and its associated guidance for statutory, private, voluntary and independent settings. These documents outline what is inspected and how, and set out expectations of practitioners and other staff, the conduct of the inspection and the format for the report.

From 2001 the inspection of all settings receiving government funding will be inspected by OFSTED, thus alleviating the need for two inspection systems within some sectors. Inspectors will include those previously inspecting under the Children Act, who will in future inspect both the curriculum and the care of children.

Advantages

- OFSTED inspection applies a framework of clear external criteria.
- The inspection system gives a national, hopefully objective overview of all settings and providers.
- Inspection provides an opportunity to have your strengths celebrated in a public report.
- OFSTED inspectors have experience over many settings and are often prepared to give informal advice as well as formal judgements.

External perspectives – inspection

'... whether the quality of teaching and curriculum development are monitored, evaluated and supported;

Whether the school, through its development planning, identifies relevant priorities and targets, takes the necessary action, and monitors and evaluates its progress towards them.'

Framework for the Inspection of Schools, OFSTED, HMSO 1995

'Inspectors must evaluate and report on what pupils achieve by 5 in nursery or reception classes with reference to
- *attainment, in the areas of learning*
- *progress in relation to prior attainment'*

Guidance on the Inspection of Nursery and Primary Schools, OFSTED, HMSO 1995

Summary

- Monitoring and evaluation is a professional activity for which we have a responsibility.
- Monitoring and evaluation should focus on the improvement of teaching and learning and result in better learning experiences for the child.
- There is a wide range of possible strategies available to us. We should practise selecting the best method to answer the questions we ask.

First Hand - making the Foundation Curriculum work

Bibliography
and
Appendices

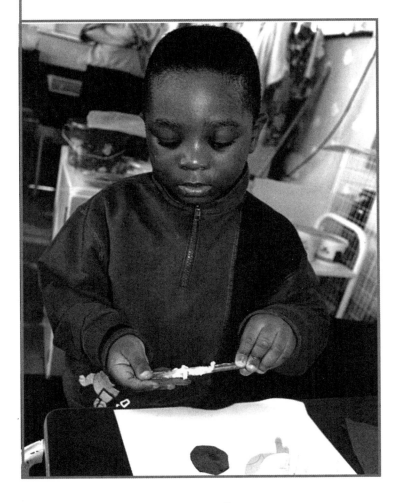

Bibliography

ALEXANDER, Robin (1995). *Versions of Primary Education*, Routledge/OUP. ISBN 0-415-12838-2

BENNETT, Neville, (1989). *A Good Start? Four Year Olds in Infant Schools*, Blackwell. ISBN 0-631-16971-7

BIRMINGHAM CITY COUNCIL, Education Department (1997). *Climbing Frames – a Framework for Learning form Birth to Five*, NFER Nelson.

CLEAVE, Shirley and BROWN, Sandra, (1991). *Early to School – Four year olds in Infant Classes* , NFER-Nelson. ISBN 07005-1269-1

CURTIS, Audrey, (1986). *A Curriculum for the Pre-school Child*, NFER-Nelson.
ISBN 0 7005 0640 3

DAVIES, Brent and ELLISON, Linda, (1994). *Managing the Effective Primary School*, Longman.
ISBN 0-582-22868-9

DAY, Chris, WHITTAKER, D., JOHNSTON, D., (1990). *Managing Primary Schools in the 1990s*, Chapman.

DEAN, Joan, (1992). *Organising Learning in the Primary School Classroom*, Routledge.
ISBN 0-415-06249-7

DES/HMI, (1989). *Aspects of Primary Education, the Education of Children Under 5*, HMSO.

DES, (1990). *Starting with Quality, Committee of Enquiry into the quality of the Educational Experience offered to 3-and 4-year olds (The Rumbold Committee Report)*, HMSO.

DfEE, (1995). *Governing Bodies and Effective Schools*, HMSO.

DfEE, (1996). *The Nursery Education Scheme – the next steps*, HMSO.

DOWLING, M, (1988). *Education 3-5, A Teacher's Handbook*, Chapman.

EARLY CHILDHOOD FORUM AND NATIONAL CHILDREN'S BUREAU (1998). *Quality in Diversity in Early Learning*, National Children's Bureau Enterprises Ltd. ISBN 1-900990-30-X

FULLAN, Michael, (1992). *Successful School Improvement*, Open University Press.
ISBN, 0-335-09575-5

GRIFFIN-BEAL, Christopher (1979). *Christian Schiller in his own words,* National Association for Primary Education.

HALL, Nigel (Ed), (1991). *Play in the Primary Curriculum*, Hodder and Stoughton.
ISBN 0-340-53805-8

HAMLYN Paul (Foundation) (1993). *Learning to Succeed: the report of the National Commission on Education*, Heinemann.

HAMLYN Paul (Foundation)/National Commission on Education (1996). *Success Against The Odds, Effective schools in disadvantaged areas*, Routledge.
ISBN 0-415-13526-5

HMI, (1989). *The Education of Children Under Five*, HMSO.
ISBN 0-11-270670-3

HMI, (1995). *The Curriculum from 5 to 16*, HMSO.
ISBN 0-11-270586-5

HMI, (1986). *Geography from 5-16, Curriculum Matters 7*, HMSO.

HMI/OFSTED, (1993). *First Class, The Standards and Quality of Education in Reception Classes*, HMSO.
ISBN 0-11-350020-3

HUGHES, Martin, (1986). *Children and Number*, Blackwell.

LEICESTERSHIRE COUNTY COUNCIL, Education Department, (1989). *A Teacher's Guide to Curriculum Review*, Leicestershire County Council.

McMILLAN, Margaret, (1919). *The Nursery School*, Dent.

MORTIMORE, Peter, (1989). *School Matters*, Open Books.
ISBN 0-7291-0194-0

NAHT (1995). *An entitlement to Quality*, NAHT.

NATIONAL CURRICULUM COUNCIL, (1989). *A Framework for the Primary Curriculum* HMSO.

OFSTED (1993). *Access and Achievement in Urban Education*, HMSO.

OFSTED (1995). *Improving Schools*, HMSO.
ISBN 0-11-350039-4

OFSTED/DFEE, (1996). *Setting Targets to Raise Standards, A survey of Good Practice*, HMSO.
ISBN 0-85522-486X

OFSTED (1995). *The Framework for the Inspection of Schools.*, HMSO (free).

OFSTED (1995). *Guidance on the Inspection of Nursery and Primary Schools*, HMSO.
ISBN 0 11 350066 1

OFSTED (1998). *Nursery Inspection Resource Pack,* HMSO. (contains Inspection Schedule, Manager's Form, Inspection Report format and Inspection Notebook).

OFSTED (1995). *Making the Most of Inspection*, HMSO.

OFSTED (1998). *School Evaluation Matters*, HMSO.

O'NEILL, John and KITSON, Neil (Ed) (1996). *Effective Curriculum Management*, Routledge.
ISBN 0-415-12409-3

PRE-SCHOOL PLAYGROUPS ASSOCIATION (1990). *Guidelines: Good practice for parent and toddler playgroups.* Pre-school Learning Alliance.

PRE-SCHOOL PLAYGROUPS ASSOCIATION (1993). *Guidelines: Good practice for sessional playgroups.* Pre-school Learning Alliance.

PRE-SCHOOL PLAYGROUPS ASSOCIATION (1993). *Guidelines: Good practice for full and extended daycare playgroups.* Pre-school Learning Alliance.

QCA/DfEE (2000) *Curriculum Guidance for the Foundation Stage* QCA publications

SCAA/QCA (1997). *Baseline Assessment, Information For Schools*, HMSO.

SCAA/DFEE (1996). *Nursery Education – the Next Steps*, HMSO. (Double pack containing *Desirable Outcomes for Children's Learning.* Available from the DfEE tel. 0345 543 3450).
ISBN 0-8552-4780

SCAA/QCA (1996). *Looking at Children's Learning, Desirable Outcomes for Children's Learning on Entering Compulsory Education*, HMSO.
ISBN 1-85838-238-6

SCAA (1995). *Planning the Curriculum at Key Stages 1 and 2*, HMSO.

SCHOOLS COUNCIL (1978). *Occasional Paper, Art 7-11*, HMSO.

TIZARD, BARBARA (1974). *Early Childhood Education*, NFER-Nelson.

VYGOTSKY (1978). *Mind and Society*, Harvard University Press.

WOLFENDALE, Sheila (1993). *Baseline Assessment, a review of current practice, issues and strategies for effective implementation*, Trentham Books.
ISBN 1-85856-009-8

Appendix 1

The Early Learning Goals (QCA 2000)

EARLY LEARNING GOALS FOR THE END OF RECEPTION YEAR (QCA)

Personal, Social & Emotional Development

* continue to be interested, excited and motivated to learn
* be confident to try new activities, initiate ideas and speak in a familiar group
* maintain attention, concentration and sit quietly when appropriate
* have a developing awareness of their own needs, views and feelings and be sensitive to the needs, views and feelings of others
* have a developing respect for their own cultures and beliefs and those of other people
* respond to significant experiences, showing a range of feelings when appropriate
* form good relationships with adults and peers
* work as part of a group or class, taking turns and sharing fairly, understanding that there need to be agreed values, and codes of behaviour for groups of people, including adults and children, to work together harmoniously
* understand what is right, what is wrong and why
* dress and undress independently and manage their own personal hygiene
* select and use activities and resources independently
* consider the consequences of their words and actions for themselves and others
* understand that people have different needs, views, cultures and beliefs, which need to be treated with respect
* understand that they can expect others to treat their needs, views, cultures and beliefs with respect

Language, Communication & Literacy

* enjoy listening to and using spoken and written language, and readily turn to it in their play and learning
* explore and experiment with sounds, words and texts
* listen with enjoyment and respond to stories, songs, and other music, rhymes and poems and make up their own stories, rhymes and poems
* use language to imagine and recreate roles and experiences
* use talk to organise, sequence and clarify thinking, ideas, feelings and events
* sustain attentive listening, responding to what they have heard by relevant comments, questions or actions
* interact with others, negotiating plans and activities and taking turns in conversations
* extend their vocabulary, exploring the meanings and sounds of new words
* retell narratives in the correct sequence, drawing on the language patterns of stories
* speak clearly and audibly with confidence and control and show awareness of the listener, for example by their use of conventions such as 'please' and 'thank you'
* hear and say initial and final sounds in words, short vowel sounds within words
* link letters and sounds, naming and sounding all letters of the alphabet
* read a range of familiar and common words and simple sentences independently
* know that print carries meaning, and in English, is read from left to right and top to bottom
* show an understanding of elements of stories, such as main character, sequence of events, openings, and how information can be found in non fiction texts, to answer questions about where, who, why and how
* attempt writing for various purposes, using features of different forms such as lists, stories, instructions
* write their own names and labels and form sentences, sometimes using punctuation
* use their phonic knowledge to write simple regular words and make phonetically plausible attempts at more complex words

First Hand - making the Foundation Curriculum work

* use a pencil effectively and hold it effectively to form recognisable letters, most of which are correctly formed

Mathematics

* say and use number names in order in familiar contexts
* count reliably up to 10 everyday objects
* recognise numerals 1-9
* use language such as more, less, greater, smaller, heavier, lighter to compare 2 numbers or quantities
* in practical activities and discussion begin to use the vocabulary involved in addition and subtraction
* find one more or one less than a number from 1-10
* begin to relate addition to combining two groups of objects, and subtraction to taking away
* talk about, recognise and recreate simple patterns
* use language such as circle, or bigger to describe the shape and size of solids and flat shapes
* use everyday words to describe position
* use mathematical ideas and methods to solve practical mathematical problems

Knowledge & Understanding of the World

* investigate objects & materials by using all of their senses as appropriate
* find out about, and identify some features of living things, objects and events they observe
* look closely at similarities, differences, patterns and change
* ask questions about why things happen and how things work
* build and construct with a wide range of objects, selecting appropriate resources, and adapting their work where necessary
* select tools and techniques they need to shape, assemble and join the materials they are using
* find out about and identify the uses of technology in their everyday lives and use computers and programmed toys to support their learning
* find out about past and present events in their own lives and in those of their families and other people they know
* observe, find out and identify features in the place they live and the natural world
* begin to know about their own cultures and beliefs & those of other people
* find out about their environment, and talk about those features they like and dislike

Physical Development

* move with confidence, imagination and in safety
* move with control and co-ordination
* show awareness of space, of themselves and others
* recognise the importance of keeping healthy and those things which contribute to this
* recognise the changes that happen to their bodies when they are active
* use a range of small and large equipment
* travel around, under, over & through balancing and climbing equipment
* handle tools, objects, construction and malleable materials safely and with increasing control

Creative Development

* explore colour, texture, shape, form & space in two and three dimensions
* recognise and explore how sounds can be changed, sing simple songs from memory, recognise repeated sounds and sound patterns and match movements to music
* respond in a variety of ways to what they see, hear, smell, touch and feel;
* use their imagination in art and design, music, dance, imaginative and role play and stories
* express and communicate their ideas, thoughts and feelings by using a widening range of materials, suitable tools, imaginative and role play, movement, designing and making, and a variety of songs and instruments

Appendix 2

aide memoire for short term planning

Successful short term planning has these features

• It identifies **the range of activities you intend to pursue during the day**. It is essential to think clearly about these since some will need careful preparation of the classroom.	• How am I going to plan my day or week?
• It **recognises the needs of individuals and groups**. Your planning will need to identify the children to whom you need to give some individual help, as well as those who will work in groups.	• Who am I planning for?
• It identifies **groupings**, whether these are for child initiated activities or those which are teacher directed.	• Which group(s) will be involved?
• It focuses on **a manageable number of objectives** for each activity.	• What do I want them to achieve – what can I reasonably hope for?
• It **identifies resources** including staffing and space.	• What will they need and who will they work with?
• It **identifies assessment criteria** and methods, using observation as a major contributor, but also including self assessment, description, questioning and outcomes in terms of artefacts and recorded tasks.	• How will I know whether the activity was successful?
• Simple, staged **objectives** are identified **for core activities** such as sand, water, books, small world play, outdoor play, etc.	• Am I recognising and valuing all activities?
• It **recognises core skills** as well as thematic or topic activities.	• Am I planning core skills activities as thoroughly as thematic ones?
• It identifies the children whose work you plan to check as part of **tracking progress** over time.	• How will I track achievement in a manageable way?
• It includes a space for **review** notes – those things which you need to remember for the next week or for individual children.	• How well did it go? Did we finish everything – are there any gaps, problems for individuals or things we should remember for next time?

Staffing Ratios for Institutions providing Nursery Education

From *Nursery Education - The Next Steps,* DfEE 1996, and based on the provision made for four year olds. Provision for younger and older children remains subject to separate requirements.

There are at present different staffing regimes for institutions providing nursery education, depending on the type of institution:

- Private and local authority day nurseries and pre-school playgroups providing full time and sessional care and education: the Department of Health's guidance for the Children Act 1989 recommends a minimum adult:child ratio of 1:8 for children between 3 and 5. At least half the staff must hold a relevant qualification in day care or education, or have completed a specified training course.

- Nursery schools and nursery classes attached to local authority maintained and grant maintained primary schools: for nursery schools where the headteacher usually teaches, DfEE circular 2/73 recommends a ratio of 2:20 (i.e. 1:10). For nursery classes. For nursery classes, it recommends 2:26 (i.e. 1:13). Half the staff, and all those employed as teachers (with limited exceptions), must have qualified teacher status.

- Private nursery schools: subject to the Children Act guidance. The recommended staffing ratios are the same as for maintained nursery schools and classes where half the staff have qualified teacher status, i.e. 1:20 or 2:26. One of the adults must have qualified teacher status and one be a qualified nursery assistant. Where more than one half are not qualified teachers, the recommended ration is 1:8 as in private day nurseries.

- Reception/infant classes in maintained schools: there is no guidance on staffing levels. Teachers have to have qualified teacher status, and may be assisted by classroom assistants.

- Nursery classes in independent schools: no guidance

The Framework for Inspecting Schools from Jan 2000

Teaching Criteria

Inspectors must evaluate and report on:

the quality of teaching, judged in terms of its impact on pupils' learning and what makes it successful or not. Inspectors must include evaluations of:

- how well the skills of literacy and numeracy are taught
- how well the school meets the needs of all its pupils, taking account of age, gender, ethnicity, capability, special needs, gifted and talented pupils, and those for whom English is an additional language
- how well pupils learn and make progress.

In determining their judgements, inspectors should consider the extent to which teachers:

- show good subject knowledge and understanding in the way they present and discuss their subject;
- are technically competent in teaching phonics and other basic skills;
- plan effectively, setting clear objectives that pupils understand;
- challenge and inspire pupils, expecting the most of them, so as to deepen their knowledge and understanding;
- use methods which enable all pupils to learn effectively;
- manage pupils well and insist on high standards of behaviour;
- use time, support staff and other resources, especially information and communication technology, effectively;
- assess pupils' work thoroughly and use assessments to help and encourage pupils to overcome difficulties;
- use homework effectively to reinforce and/or extend what is learned in school;

and the extent to which pupils:

- acquire new knowledge or skills, develop ideas and increase their understanding;
- apply intellectual, physical or creative effort in their work;
- are productive and work at a good pace;
- show interest in their work, are able to sustain concentration and think and learn for themselves;
- understand what they are doing, how well they have done and how they can improve

from **The Handbook for Inspecting Primary and Nursery Schools from Jan 2000.**

'*Growth is a process of change which we can apprehend as a pattern; not as a pattern like that on a hearthrug, fixed until it is worn through, but a pattern like that of a sunrise, changing continuously in space and time, and similar but never the same from one day to the next. We do not hold a sunrise still on a pin, and measure its dimensions. What is of concern in a sunrise is its quality.*'

Christian Schiller, 1895 – 1976